PRAISES FOR

The Blossoming Woman

This book helped me to recognize the power that often lies dormant within each of us and that alone was powerful.

— Ardre Orie

Bryann's realistic writing style, helped me to denounce societal imposed standards and learn to just be myself.

— Madelyn Jensen

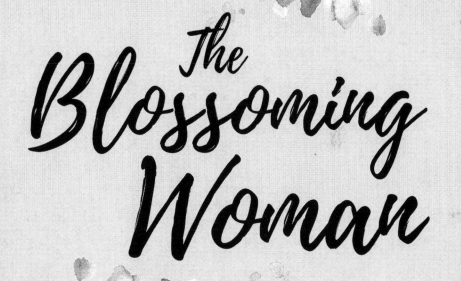

The Blossoming Woman

BRYANN ANDREA

WWW.13THANDJOAN.COM

Dedication

To all the *wildflowers* amongst a
universe that only sees beauty in roses.
Your space and place in this world is
undeniable.

Epigraph

The *day* rose when the risk to remain comfortable in a bud was more *painful* than the risk it took to *blossom*.

Table of Contents

Introduction

When you think of "The Blossoming Woman", I'm sure you're imagining sunshine, rainbows, and maybe a little glitter gleaming from the sky as this woman is sprouting to become this conspicuous flower. Well, you're partially right, but you're missing a few things - the storms, rain, cold, and being carried through this world by someone who doesn't exactly have a "green thumb".

Would you believe me if I told you that I had no intent of making this a book? I started writing "The Blossoming Woman" in 2010. During that time, I endured a lot of growing pains. I was dealing with abandonment, heartbreak, and suffering from severe depression and anxiety. For years, I didn't know who I was or what I'd grow to become because physically and mentally rising out of that environment seemed impossible. It felt like I went from not being watered enough to drowning - all because I did not know how to cope or properly nourish myself through these adversities. Picking up a pen and telling my truth was one of the best things I could have ever done for myself. It saved my life. What is now a book started off as a personal journal of entries I'd write to myself for a source of encouragement and hope. I would share bits and pieces of my entries across differ-ent platforms and what I found surprised me. There were other women that had grown through it or were currently growing through it. There were other women, like me, who were trying to navigate through a personal space of trauma and unknowing. There were women pouring back into me for sharing my truth - something I was once ashamed and afraid to do. They were receptive, and my words were helping - to some, even healing. In those moments, I realized a need for a space that allowed us, women, to not only survive, but to thrive in our truth. I realized my untold story of overcoming was no longer a story solely for me.

On a mission to water myself, I was creating a network of women who selflessly watered each other. It was time for me to take my rightful place in the garden. It was time for me to have a healthy self-respect, bal-anced self-love, and a firm, unshakable confidence in myself and the gifts, talents, and abilities I would soon discover. Now, it is time for you. Easier said than done, but prayerfully after digesting this reading for your per-sonal nourishment, you will realize, you too are The Blos-soming Woman. A woman who is ready to discover. A woman who understands in order to conquer the world, she must conquer herself. A woman who is ready to live boldly and fearlessly in her truth.

Writing these words brought out some of the most beautiful and ugly pieces of my past There were as many smiles as there were tears. It was an intervention I didn't ask for, butI I needed it badly. It became therapeutic in a way that allowed me to release and re-plant myself. It helped me create boundaries, have faith, and put self-care at the forefront of my living.

These words will nourish you, charge you to plant seeds that you never thought to plant before, enable you to weather storms, and give you the courage to rise up and grow through it.

I'm a living testimony that our environments have little to nothing to do with our destinations. It doesn't matter what's around, your focus should be on what is within. If you are planted in a great environment, but are in a terrible headspace, odds are you will conquer nothing. I don't believe in bad seeds. I just believe in bad gardeners. Growing, wherever you may be, will require a lot of nourishment. Since you have picked up this book, I know that indicates a dedicated commitment you are willing to make to yourself.

1
Seed Planting

"Plants do not spring up where no seeds were planted. What you plant in the soil of *hopes and dreams,* you will reap in harvest season. There are *no gardening mistakes.* Plant wherever you land. Even in the most infertile of lands, seeds that are planted with faith and love will *grow.*"

"Learning is the *beginning* of all things - It's the beginning of life, health, wealth, and the spirituality of the fruits of learning. Searching and learning are where the *magic begins*."

FRESH START

*B*e thankful that you are present in your physical and spiritual being. Despite whatever good or bad that has occurred in your life, let today be your fresh start. You will choose to smile because you are still holding on to something so precious that not everyone is guaranteed- life. You will finally decide to let go of what has been burdening you for so long. You will take this day to breathe and digest what it is you actually want out of life. Some people are so consumed in the thought that the new year is the only day to realign, plan, and get to it. Every day we wake up is the day we have an opportunity to elevate.and Learn about your needs and wants. Dig deep and consider any habits that you either need to implement or dismiss. Most importantly, think about your goals. You may or may not have gotten around to executing all you set out to do, but if you're reading this I hope you know that you still have time. This is your fresh start to set out to do all you desire. Think about some areas where you may have fallen short and try to be more strategic this time around. Think about what has worked for you and continue to do so. I encourage you to write down your goals, give yourself a reasonable deadline, and when finished, speak it into existence! Actually tell yourself "this will happen" or "I will do this". Put your list of goals in a very visual space so that you will see it and be reminded everyday. Learning is the beginning of life. when you are able to learn about yourself, it makes life so much more enjoyable because you are able to live freely and be firm in who you are. Go after that job you want, paint that picture, plant your garden, confess your love, get your degree, buy that house, write that book. The only thing standing in the way of you is you, but today is your fresh start!

"Only dreams come *true* when there is action behind *them*."

ALLOW YOURSELF TO DREAM

One of the most frustrating cases amongst us is that we don't know what we want to do with our life. A part of me would like to believe it's because of the endless possibilities life has to offer us. We don't know what it is we want to be passionate about because we aren't able to pinpoint it to just one thing. We continuously search for something that makes us happy and fulfills us, but at the same time we are mindful of the expectations and pressure society puts on us. All of us have dreams, but not all of us choose to wholeheartedly pursue them. We give up or life gets in the way. I've been there. I've created plenty of excuses in my head to reason why I didn't go after my dreams. The truth is I was being lazy, frightened, or my life actually did get in the way. It started off with smaller dreams. Dreams that many would consider to be in reach! I was so shrunken in fear that I would attempt, not follow through, and be stuck in the pains of "what if?" It would then lead me to not allow myself to dream any further because of the emotional consequences I'd face if my dreams didn't come true. I was inhibiting my own imagination. We have to find a medium that allows us to dream. We have to create a safe place inside of us that combats fear. Tell yourself "It's okay for me to dream. I am allowed to. I will make small efforts day by day until my dreams become reality. I am only limited by the thoughts of my mind." We don't have to make massive changes in our every-day life to watch our dreams unfold into a reality, but sometimes we do. What are you dreaming of right now? Write it down. Dreams are not meant to pain you, but make you excited about life. Dreams give us a reason to wake up everyday and get after it. After all, we only have one life to live - so allow yourself to dream and be in good spirits doing so.

"There is no *challenge* more challenging than the challenge to be a better *you*."

CHALLENGE YOURSELF

*C*hallenging ourselves on a regular basis brings about certainty to the success in our lives. When we challenge ourselves, we are entering into the space of the unknown. Entering into that space usually comes with discomfort, risk, and not knowing. If you never make it a point to challenge yourself, you will only know what is familiar. You will never know the creativity and ingenuity within you unless you challenge yourself to discover the skill sets beyond those you've already acquired.Get out of the routine of waking up, doing your jobs, and coming home to go to sleep. That type of repetitiveness dulls you. Is there something you would like to be doing outside of your job? One of my friends worked as a banker, but he had a serious love for fashion. He, like many of us, went to work, came home to rest, and did it all over again. One day he went out on a limb and actually quit his job to pursue his fashion ambitions full time. What a risk! Needless to say, he challenged himself and fully invested into his dreams, and now he is designing full time and using his creative direction for multiple projects. I'm not telling you to go out and quit your job but make time for the things that you really want to do.

Challenge yourself to get out of the cycle of routinely being alive and actually push to live a more vibrant life. For we only have one life to live. Do what you love and love what you do!

"Don't judge each day by the *fruits,*
but by the *seeds* that you plant - by the
bricks that you lay.

SEED PLANTING

*T*o grow the garden within us, we have to prepare the soil. We have to make furrows in our life for the seeds we want to see bloom. Time will lapse before we are fully able to reap the rewards of our gardens. There is work to be done in your growth process. We need to be planted in good soil and nourished with love and water. Our roots have to be sternly planted so that we are able to weather the winds, the rain, and the cold. Life works the same way. We can't expect a harvest if we've never adequately planted a seed. We can't expect an immediate harvest after the seed planting. All we can do is put forth our works to assure the seeds will grow — to assure we will grow and reap the harvest from our deliberate seed planting. When my garden wasn't growing, it took establishing myself in a better area to fully flourish. I took 2017 to plant seeds because I expected to reap the harvest in 2018. It came with organizing my rows, tending, and weeding. To get more specific and literal; it took a lot of self love. Enough self-love that helped me to let go of anything that was hindering my growth. During the time it took me to bloom, it wasn't always an eye souring development. There were times and spaces that were unproductive. Needless to say, invest in yourself and trust that your personal maturation will be a reflection of the works, planting, and sowing you've savored. Seed plant in the current year. Reap the harvest in the following year, but start planting now.

"My deepest *fear* is losing myself and turning into what everybody expects *me to be.*"

LIVE UP TO YOUR OWN EXPECTATIONS

We can no longer live our life ceaselessly trying to meet the standards of people who are most likely incapable of being pleased. That is a sure path to a regretful existence. We have to make our own way based on who we are, what interest us, our needs, and what we value. Let us push the envelope past existence – we want to live. There is no obligation to live up to anyone's expectations no matter who is pushing them on you. We do things as human beings because we are interested and caring, and it feels like the right thing to do. Being the new woman at my job, I instantly wanted everyone to like me. I even went to great lengths to change some things that came naturally to me to appease some of my peers. It started to get in the way of my "why". Why did I start this job? Certainly not to be the "liked by everybody" employee, but to get the job done. Expectations have a way of watering down our experiences in life. If we follow our own way and make mistakes along the way, we get to learn from our mistakes without the ridicule from third parties. Nobody knows us better than we know ourselves, therefore, we should be better able to decide our own destiny. Allow yourself the freedom to speak your truth and be who you are. Cut out the fear of being contained by opinions and be who you are because that's enough. It will always be enough.

"Even in the *dawn* you can
feel a little *light*."

FAITH IS FUEL

*O*ur faith is what moves mountains while our doubts can create them. Faith is the primary fuel to all of our aspirations, struggles, and even our dreams. Faith is the key to opening up our doors of optimism and opportunity. It is what makes us feel that we can and that we are able. Faith is what comes from believing. In life, we can be certain that there will be both good and bad times. If I am to be honest with you, Instead of having faith that everything was going to work out for my greater good, during a lot of my bad times, I spent wondering "why me?". For me, my faith is a direct result of believing in God. As a matter of fact, a lot of the invaluable life lessons I will continue to share with you are what I have learned on my walk with Christ. We may not be taking the same walk, and that is okay – but in almost every religion, we share the same practice of having faith. Putting our complete trust or confidence in something and expecting the best outcome despite how we may feel in the moment is what it means to have faith. If you are currently experiencing something that isn't panning out to your expectations, do whatever it is you can about it, and have faith that things will turn around for you. Faith without works is dead.

"*Passion* is what fuels you to do something *great*."

PASSION IS THE FRUIT OF LIFE

Some of you may have heard the phrase, "when you do what you love, you won't have to work a day in your life." Have you really taken the time to break down what that means? When we are vested in careers that make our hearts full, the work doesn't feel so much like work anymore. It feels natural and like a way of life. I had a friend who did executive banking, but had an interest in fashion and design. He would go to work every day, mind in one place, and heart in the other. I had another friend in the same field of work, but was more interested in photography. She could only book so many gigs because her main priority was her banking job. When you get stuck doing something you feel "you have to do" for whatever reasons, life gets a little dull and feels a little more routine. Needless to say, both of them walked away from banking to invest in their passions. The new found radiance and positivity were very apparent for the both of them. When we do what we love, every day feels like a blessing. The joy it brings to us spills out into other areas of our life. If it's a matter of figuring out what makes you tick or what you're genuinely passionate about, take some time to do that. Worry less about security and obligations and focus on the love you have within. Go after your passion and bear the fruit!

"Consider your *plan* like a personal road map. All you need is the *courage* to press on to your destination."

CREATE A PLAN

For many of us, putting our ideas down and organizing a plan are the easy steps. The hard part is actually doing it and figuring out where to begin. I've been there. Like all projects, we can get overwhelmed with all of the tedious tasks we take on to run anything functional. We get stuck in being such perfectionist that it stalls the time we take to actually put out our work. Of course, that is not necessarily a bad thing, but for the over the top perfectionist like myself, it can sometimes get in the way. So much that much time has passed and either we let that plan go or we aren't as enthused when it's time to deliver. To keep me on the right track, I have always made it a habit to set some type of deadline. We all start with a vision. Through that vision we come up with our mission and purpose. In the midst of that, we set some goals and a reasonable time frame to meet those goals. Plan some different strategies to achieve those goals and finalize your vision and purpose, and then put it into action. We can never forget or stray from putting the plan into action. After that is complete, we have our beginner's guide to what I would like to call our business plans. Not only create the plan, but start making a solid initiative to follow through with the plans you make. I have learned that lack of resources or funds is no longer an excuse in this era when we have technology on our side. Get creative and create a plan. You'll be surprised where it could take you.

"By doing what we *love*, we never ever work a day in our *life*."

CAREER
CONSCIOUS

*T*here is a constant tug of war between doing what we love and ensuring we are in a career where we will be financially secure.

The question posed is if we are really passionate about what we love to do, but it doesn't really make us a lot of money, do we still do it? My answer is yes as much as it is no. When we enter high school, college, or are fresh on our way out – we tend to live in an area of unknown for a while. We don't know exactly what it is we want to do, but we are certain of the things that make us tick and bring light to our lives. At that point, do we go for it? Yes! At that stage, you don't really have a lot of financial bindings or many dependents. So you have a little free range to do what it is you want to do. If you're in a situation where you need to put a greater emphasis on making ends meet, then picking a career choice that protects your economic life is the better route. You have bills, mouths to feed, and rent due – go ahead and get the career that secures the bag. This doesn't mean that you can't put seconds, minutes, and hours into your passions because you totally can. You totally should. I used to work selling resident security systems. There was no way I could've seen myself doing that long term, but I needed a steady income. When we have opportunities throughout the day to get a little closer to our dreams, take full advantage.

"Don't let anything *stand* in your way of claiming better. We will only manifest in the life we choose rather than the life we *experience* by default."

CLAIMING THE VICTORY

*T*here is a special ability within you to speak things into reality. The tongue is a powerful tool, and the words you speak matter. Tread lightly and declare positive occurrences. Are you being mindful of the different convictions you are making over your life? Do you notice yourself saying "I can't" more than "I will?." There are convincing factors in each statement. When you allow those "I can't" thoughts to rummage in your mind, you will eventually believe it. When you believe you can't do something, it takes away your willpower to even try. Then we are left with the pains of wondering "what if?" Once you start speaking things into existence and claiming the victory, your habits will change. You will convince yourself you can, and you'll start to subconsciously make tangible efforts to ensure that you will. We are only limited by the barriers and boundaries of our thoughts. When you speak in a specific way of proclaiming your desires, the universe will listen and deliver. Claiming your victory is like giving yourself permission to succeed. The truth is, sometimes you may not claim your victories because you are too on yourself. I thought twice about writing this book because of how disappointed I would be if I didn't finish it. What got to me, was how upset I would be at the fact that I didn't even try. I got in my car that day, heading to work, and at a stop light I started telling myself "I will write that book. I will finish it and get it published." We have gotten in the pattern of beating ourselves up over shortcomings and failures, but in reality that is how life fluctuates. Not every battle will be won, but who's to say we can't indulge in every battle? When you have a deep conviction, you are grateful to be alive, you are grateful that you can even try, you're not focused on the naysayers or what's going wrong. Unapologetically, claim your victory, do your works, and have some faith. Speak what you want in this life until you are able to see what you said. When that time comes, when you are able to see your victories, claim more victories. We are only limited by the things we think we can and cannot do.

"Financial *freedom* is spending
what is left after *saving*."

POCKET YOUR PENNIES

*T*he very first time I was able to understand monetary value, I felt the pressure of saving. Can you recall your parents bribing you with a few dollars or even change and shortly after telling you to "save it for a new toy or some candy"? We actually do it because now we have something to put our saving efforts towards. Adulthood similarly works the same way. I've been in the habit of spending it when I have it and then getting it right back – I wish I hadn't been. There are so many reasons to save. Saving money can give us a peace of mind. The more we save, the easier it gets to save additional money. I know that may sound funny at first, but just hear me out. As we save, our financial worries seem less and less. If you've ever been in a situation where your hours are cut short and you need to compensate because rent is due, how good would it feel to have that emergency funding available to you in your savings? Savings reduce our stress, and now we have more energy to invest in more enjoyable thoughts and activities. Saving gives us options. It puts us in control of our own destiny. We can move, take some time to find a new job, put a downpayment on a new car. Most importantly, saving gives us the option to invest in ourselves and our dreams. Start that business, write that book, and travel. Yes, I know that when we die the money we have worked so hard to save is not coming with us. I hear you. There are huge, stressful psychological influences that can occur from living check to check. It might mean passing up on a few of those new shirts or sneakers we really want, but it is totally worth it when we are rewarded with not only peace of mind, but an opportunity to build something up in order for us to branch out. Pocket your pennies.

"Surround *yourself* with people who will contribute to your *elevation*."

HUDDLE UP

*I*n every aspect of our lives, we are in the midst of some sort of team. I'm not talking solely athletics, but these teams can be built from family, peers at work, church, or in our social clubs. Even as an entrepreneur, it is our duty to form some type of team to distribute the work and remain on a solid system. I would like to consider our teams to be something like our support systems. These are the people we turn to when things are great, we want to tell them all about it. These are the people we turn to when things are bad, we want them there to listen and comfort us. These are the people we bring together for support and encouragement. This team will be present in both good and bad times. We huddle with our team during our times of need, clarity, and success. The huddle is so necessary from an innovative standpoint. Next time you watch an athletic event, pay close attention to the team when they huddle. What does that look like? What does that sound like? I see men and women who in that moment are physically leaning on one another and supporting each other. They are making sure all of their visions are in alignment – everyone wants to win. They are encouraging each other to push on through briefing with positive affirmations. I don't think it's any different from what we do with our personal teams. Especially during our time of fatigue, it is important to huddle up. When we break from that huddle, we are mentally prepared to get back out there on that line of scrimmage and win. Don't just surround yourself with people for the sake of it, but align yourself with visionaries that will be vested in your success and ready to huddle up.

"Measure your net worth not by how much you *have*, but by how many people you *impact and connect* with."

YOUR NETWORK IS YOUR NET WORTH

Make an effort to go to networking events, socialize, and volunteer. You never know the people you might meet and the connections you'll make along the way. Sometimes who you know gets you just as far or even further than what you know! While in college, I had the opportunity to serve on former president Barack Obama's White House Initiative on HBCUs (Historically Black Colleges and Universities). It was truly a privilege and one of the biggest honors of my life. It was through an application process in which I was selected, and it took a lot of guts for me to do that. I mean, come on, it's President Barack Obama! I could only imagine the pool of talented HBCU students I'd be up against. Nonetheless, I was selected and was able to attend the conference in Washington D.C. I missed some basketball practices in order to do so, but the impact of this opportunity would last me forever. I could not miss it! In the midst of the conference, they had a "job hunt" session where employers would come from Fortune 500 companies to talk to us. I am one of the most introverted "blue" people on earth. It really took a lot of self motivation to get me out there and rolling with what I considered the "big wigs". Luckily, I had business cards. I met a director of one of two of the most popular grocery store chains in America who eventually offered me a marketing position in their corporate office. I met entrepreneurial investors. Most importantly, I met my other HBCU All Stars. They lit a fire in me!. I wanted to know all eighty one of them, who they were, where they were from, and what they wanted out of life. I had peers who wrote grants, worked in public relations, STEM, and interned with government official.. I was so intrigued by how multifaceted we all were and the endless possibilities ahead when we were all able to put our heads together. Many of us from that one conference were either hired on the spot or eventually hired by the many fortune 500 companies that were present. Networking provided an opportunity for us to step out of our comfort zones and put a little effort into getting out there and meeting people.. In moments of opportunity, sometimes we find ourself set back by the fear of rejection and the possibility of not being able to relate or connect. There is more damage in not trying than trying and not succeeding. It takes a village to build an empire. So finding your tribe is necessary.

"Winning is *good*, but having that desire to win is even *better*."

WOMEN WIN

There are a lot of women out there who are gifted in several areas, but never accomplish anything. Tim Grover states "the body has limitations that the mind does not. We spend so much time focusing on what's happening from the neck down, and we forget it all starts in our head." We are never really physically prepared if we are not mentally ready. If we aren't mentally ready, we aren't ready at all. Few people really achieve a high level of success because they never get past the dreaming and goal setting phase. Women who win are motivated to at least try. We all have a gift, but it is up to us to tap into it. Most people think winning is routed on a straight path. They follow the pecking order and then expect everything to be guaranteed. Go to high school, go to college, get a job, and everything will be alright. That's not how it works. Once you decide you want something, that imaginary straight line then transforms into something "squiggly." That's what the path to winning looks like. Nothing worth it ever came easy, but women are qualified and more than capable. Nothing extraordinary ever became of my life until I realized how extraordinary I am. Winning is a campaign of hard work, but the power to win is within.

"Life should be a *continuous* source of *inspiration*."

FIND YOUR INSPIRATION

Books have helped plant seeds in my soul. Books have always given me the inspiration that one day I would rise out of the environment that could've easily held me back. Books are like the water to my thoughts – nourishing me with the confidence to dream and transcend all barriers. A huge part of dreaming is finding your inspiration. Books allow me to explore hidden realms and better understand people that do not connect with me or my experiences. I used to be into self-help books for a while. Then I got into history and autobiographies of people like Oprah Winfrey, Frida Kahlo, and Mahatma Gandhi. I included reading an autobiography of Sam Walton – the man who built Walmart from the ground up in a small town of about 2,500 people. Exploring the people and history of unfamiliarity inspires me to leave my comfort zone. There's incredible power, knowledge, and inspiration that be discovered once you tap into an interest to better understand the world and people unfamiliar to you. We can't limit ourselves by only learning from people like us. If it's authentic and interesting, tap into it. The way you find inspiration could be totally different from how I find mine, but there is no wrong or right way to find inspiration. I would just advise you to look for it beyond the people and things that look like you. We don't stand so united because our disinterested in learning about one another. Be inspired by the dreamers because they provoke you to go out and learn more, do more, and become more.

"Real dreams seem *impossible* at first glance. It is when you summon the will; they become *inevitable*."

DREAM BIG QUEEN

*O*nce upon a time we were all little girls with big dreams. We have made promises to ourselves that one day we'd make them all come true and live in the luxury of all of our hard work. I think as we get older, the "dreamer" in us fades. Why is that? Why don't we allow ourselves to imagine and dream beyond our current realities? Is it the ridicule you might receive from other adults if you fail? Are your dreams "too big"? Do you even believe you can? Honestly, that's where it starts – it starts within us. Our ability to dream is permitted by the dreamer, that's you. Your imagination will stretch as far as you allow it. Nothing is really out of reach until you think it is. The mind has a way of shackling us with prohibiting thoughts. There are plenty of ways and many connections that you haven't made yet that will assist you in fulfilling your dreams. I always dreamed of going to college, but I didn't think too much into it because of my situation at home. I knew we couldn't afford it. I was moments away from enlisting and putting everything behind me. What changed? I got in touch with the right people and did everything that I possibly could behind the scenes to assure in the end I would get some type of scholarship and be on my way. It's never our environment that inhibits our goals and dreams, it is the dreamer.

"Remember that sometimes
not getting what you want is a
good thing."

FOOL'S GOLD

The things we want may not be what we really need. They sometimes come as distractions and are dressed up as everything we desire. These items are the things that feel good, but are not exactly good for us. I like to call this fool's gold. It comes in many shapes, sizes, colors, and even in human form. You can find yourself in a frenzy when you don't get the things that you want. Perhaps you find yourself calling out to the most high to make things "right" and fulfill these wants. I've found myself in similar situations for several reasons. Fool's gold might manifest itself in the unknowing, relationship issues, career clarity, family problems, and in one hundred and one reasons. We have to really digest a few things here. First, there is a reason for everything whether it goes our way or not. Nothing happens to us on accident. I am a firm believer in that. Next, we have to trust that if it's meant for us, it will be. Lastly, time heals all, and whatever has left us or whatever has never been fulfilled will be replaced by something much bigger and perhaps even better. We don't always get the things we want, but we can expect that something better is on the way. Let us not be fooled by the fool's gold.

"*Money* can't buy you life or
happiness."

CREAM

Have you ever heard of the saying "cash rules everything around me?" Most of us can relate to how cash actually rules everything around us from the bills to whatever else we have to purchase, but can you relate to it internally ruling you? I recall being in positions where I was living check to check, but then I realized there are people out there who are making ends meet with little to no check at all. Money isn't everything. We can't give currency so much control over our lives. I hear people teetering on the thought that money can buy happiness all the time. Of course we can't deny that the economy and society we live in romanticize money, but there are limits. What can't you buy with money? We can't buy friends, love and family. I remember moving to Kentucky and just starting my career. It was enough for me to get by on my own, but when my boyfriend graduated, he decided to move down here also. He was still trying to get grounded in his career which required me to take on all of the responsibilities. He helped where he could, but we were literally stretching. I thought that more money meant that we'd be more comfortable and that we'd be happier, but I was wrong. We were never poor or struggling as long as we had each other. We are forever rich in the company of people that we love. That will always be something money can't buy.

"Time is *short* and distractions are *plentiful*."

PUT THE PHONE DOWN!

When I was In high school my math teacher looked at me, and she looked at my phone. She then told me "that thing is going to ruin you someday". All of this technology that has allowed us to be connected to one another is nothing short of brilliant. We are in the era of complete tech savvy-ness, and it's only advancing. A lot of the things we depend on in the world are digital, but it's a poor excuse as to why we are most times glued to our gadgets. I get it; they're handy tools when it comes to our jobs, calendars, calculators, and everything else. We are doing ourselves a favor when we power off and put the phone down. All of these phones and social advancements have made us a lot less social. We depend on status updates, tweeting, and texting to thoroughly communicate. A lot of things can be mis-interpreted that way! When I am on my phone, I never realize how long I've actually been on it until hours have passed, and I'm asking myself where all the time went. I could've been exercising, cleaning up, or just doing something productive in general. I don't think we realize how distracted we really are by our phones. Let's start living without always having to document what it is we are doing. We've become more observant of others than we are of ourselves.. When we are in the moments of pure bliss, there will be no need for a phone.

"You can be the *prettiest*, most wonderful smelling flower in the world - there will still be someone who hates *flowers.*"

DO IT FOR YOU

*G*allivanting through our success treks gets interesting. People will see you doing the works and doing good work. They will acknowledge, applaud, and reward you. While all that is nice, make sure you are sticking to your core of pursuit. Not for the shine, not for the accolades – make sure you are doing it for you. When we operate with purpose and out of genuinity, we do it with determination in our souls. I understand positive reinforcement, but we can't let the lack of deter us from our purpose. Everyday I hear something new about millennials and how we only get involved in things that have a check or reward attached to it. The truth is, we have to remain intrinsically motivated which means we are doing things out of pure enjoyment or for the love of it. If we become motivated by extrinsic matter, then everything we do will be controlled by factors outside ourselves. I never want anything beyond what is within to control my pursuit of life and neither should you.

"Who cares what the world *needs*? Do what makes you come alive. Because what the world needs is people who have come *alive*."

DO IT ANYWAY

*E*ntrepreneurialism is a beautiful thing – a very risky venture, but rewarding. To be a woman standing on her own two feet in any industry or avenue of her own takes heart. Going out on a limb wasn't the scariest thing for me when I began my book writing venture. The scariest part for me was when I realized I'm going to invest in a women's empowering book when there are thousands already out there – and they're actually pretty darn good! Here's a confession, a lot of the things I've had thoughts about doing have already been done – "overly saturated" industries if you will, but if that stops us on our pursuits, we must ask if we really wanted it to begin with? When I go into a grocery store and I am looking for the barbecue sauce, there is only one barbecue sauce I will purchase. I notice that there is a large selection of barbecue sauces I could choose from, but I'm choosing one of them specifically because I know it's different from the rest – in my eyes, better! Each of us is distinctly different and made with great detail. With that being said, none of us will produce the same work. We not only possess the ability to produce this unique work, but there's a possibility we will reach or make an impact on people in ways that have yet to be done. Nothing can negate you from pursuing your dreams if you want it as bad as you think you do. Social media has been invented and reinvented for decades. Don't let the industries deter you from putting a foot through the door because those are steps that you have an opportunity to leave on someone's heart. Start your clothing line, hair company, cosmetic line, organization, book, or do whatever it is you may want to do. If it has already been done, do it anyway. I guarantee you; no one will be able to do it like you.

"Finding that *core* truth within yourself is the greatest spiritual *attainment* you can ever have."

SEVEN SEEDS

While in college, I interned with a marketing and event organizing agency that help brands discover their core truth. Branding has always been one of my favorite elements of work because it makes my creative juices flow. I always thought it was interesting how much detail and artistry go into the strategic planning of sharing brand missions, purpose, and truths. When discovering our personal truths, one of the most important questions we can ask ourselves is "what do I love to do?" If you didn't get paid for it and wouldn't do it anymore, I don't think it might be something that you love. Try picking something else. It has to be something that would inspire you every day. It has to come naturally to us – almost as natural as breathing. Do you get lost in time doing this or is this something that while you're doing it, you are constantly watching the clock? Then, is there a way you could spin this to generate income? If you were unable to relate or answered no to any of these, move on to something else on your list of things you love. Cognition of our core truth can only help us become aware of how to adequately use our gifts and share them with the universe. Take the time to figure out your core truth.

"Keep your face to the *sunshine*, and it'll almost be impossible to see the *dark*."

POWER OF POSITIVITY

*T*he mind is the most powerful tool in the body – especially when we fill it with positivity. When we change our thoughts, we will also be able to see our lives change . There is so much power in positivity. It allows us to feel powerful, empowered, and most of all limitless. What consumes your mind has the potential to control your life. That's why we have talked a great deal about being conscious of the ways that we communicate with ourselves and others. We'll never be able to pour into our lives with empty cups. No longer allow negative thoughts to linger. They will only drain your energy. Instead, focus on all the good in your life. You may not be exactly where you want to be, but look how far you've come. Think it, feel it, and speak positive affirmations over your life on a daily basis. It allows us to send positive energy into the world, and we will reap all of the wonderful things we attract. Positive thinking can only lead us to powerful outcomes.

"Our deepest *fear* is that we are more powerful than we can even *fathom*."

RETRAIN
THE BRAIN

*T*he molecular structure of the brain is designed to stop us from doing anything that could potentially hurt us, frighten us, or embarrass us. We are not designed to do things that are uncomfortable or bring us uncertainty because our brain is designed to do what it thinks to protect us. There are times it is inhibiting us from exploration in order for us to be able to do extraordinary things in our lives and businesses to fulfill our dreams. Women can expect to run into trials and difficult times. I remember being seven years old and being told to sing for Ja Rule because I was who my management thought could be the youngest member of his label at the time. Something took over my body. There I stood, in front of him, like a deer in headlights. My lips wouldn't move, and before I knew it, he was gone. Fear ran through every inch of my flesh. Today, I still think about what happened that day. It felt like my brain "abandoned ship" at the first sign of distress. As wonderful and intricate as our minds are, the brain is not always on our side. Don't allow the brain to take you out of what could be a game changer in your life. Ignore the fear, ignore the potential embarrassment, and just set your heart on trying. Exploration is what allows us to evolve – blossom

"Age is only a limitation of the *mind*"

AGE WITH GRACE

When I became an adult, I wish I hadn't wished so many times to be an adult. I wish I had focused more on positive aging than anti-aging. I wish I had known that part of growing old can get a little boring. Aging happens whether we are afraid of it or not, but when we can live, we must do so. Society places a lot of stereotypes on aging. Boobs come at this age. You're supposed to graduate by this age. Be married by this age or be miserable forever. It's all a lie. Ignore all the ridiculous unspoken age laws, and just put your focus into aging with grace. Age is only a number. I don't think it should take away from what we can or can no longer do. It's not a restriction because it is never too late to do more with the life we're given. I hear a lot of women who reach certain ages and say "well, I guess I can't do this anymore" when they secretly still want to and are in the shape to do it. I believe in the chirpy old tales that tell us age is just a state of mind. It's a trick we play on ourselves that end up dulling us down and scooting us out of the way. I was talking to one of my good friends, Laura, about this, and she had put it into the simplest of terms by saying that "we are the age of our spirits." My father is in his 60's, has a six pack, and we can't tell him to put on a shirt; I don't think we should. Live how you feel. How old would you be if you didn't know how old you are?

"What lies *behind* us and what lies ahead of us don't compare to what lives *within* us."

EVERYTHING IS WITHIN

All the powers we need are within. We as humans are one of the most highly evolved out of all living things. All of the power, freedom, and divinity are within. Well, how do we let it out? Why isn't it out already? It is not out because we don't believe. You have to whole-heartedly believe in your powerfulness and your great-ness for it to surface. You will only tap into these powers when you have a little faith in yourself. The yogi has told us that power lies within your soul. By controlling the mind and body, we are able to conquer the world by the power of our souls. It is often the only thing stand-ing in the way of your destiny, and it is you. Until you, without a doubt, believe in your own nobility, value, and virtue – there will always be a void in your spirit and a void in your soul. You are powerful beyond measure. You are beautiful. You are worthy. Within us lives infinite power and infinite potential. Your mind and spirit will only believe what you tell it. So feed it with truth, with love, and with faith. We are extremely powerful when we know how powerful we are.

2
Nourish

"*Self love* isn't narcissistic, egotistical, or selfish. Self love is the oil that fuels and rejuvenates your spirit. It's essential to your *survival* and well-being. The way that you treat your mind, body, and soul is a direct reflection of how you feel about *yourself*."

"The woman you see in the mirror - that's your *best friend*. When you're looking for love, compassion, and support, *find it in yourself*."

BE YOUR OWN FRIEND

I once was scrolling across my timeline on twitter, and a woman I was following asked "if you had a friend that talked to you in the manner that you talk to yourself, how long would you and that person be friends?" That really put things into perspective for me. Sometimes we can be so harsh on ourselves. I consider myself to be the toughest critic in my life. I think it's both a gift and a curse on how much of a perfectionist I am, but do I really deserve the harsh words and thoughts that surface to my mind when I fall short of my perfections? No, I don't – and neither do you. Growing up, I was always the stand out in my social circles and not for the most attractive reasons. I was awkward, pudgy, and enjoyed being an introvert. People on the outside influenced me into thinking I wasn't enough, and for a while I believed it and started treating myself as so. It is so easy for us to acknowledge the things we don't like, the matter we still have to work on, and the things we wish were different about ourselves. But, what about the things we like? Acknowledge those too! Acknowledge the things you already like about yourself, your accomplishments, accolades, your growth, and I bet you could come up with a lot more if you just took a minute to think about all of the good that you already possess on the inside. There is an exercise I started doing early on where I would stand in front of the mirror and for a moment I would just take in my whole reflection. Later, I would force myself to point out at least 10 things I liked about myself including interpersonal attributes. Later, I made this a ritual. I started standing bare in my mirror every morning. I even came up with a mantra "In this moment I accept myself. I am enough. " Not only was there a personal healing benefit there, but I began to trust myself. Decision making started becoming a lot easier because I developed a self instinct. I was starting to become somebody I actually liked to listen to. My thoughts felt wholesome. I was finally starting to develop the self-love that I was so badly missing for years. Whatever way you go about confirming positive affirmations within, please make it habitual, and please make it a priority. Sometimes, life feels lonely because one of the most important friends you are missing is yourself.

"A *safe space* cultivates a safe learning environment. It gives you an opportunity to *discover you.*"

CREATE A
SAFE SPACE

A safe space is usually a place free of judgment, people, and noise. This is a place where we can go to breathe, think, and unwind. When I was a child, I can recall my first ever safe space being in my closet. It was so spacious, quiet, and no one would ever think to look for me in there. As I grew older, I would escape at the park across the street from my childhood home – Roosevelt Park to be exact. There was a hill there and the top of the hill provided a place for me to sit or lay.. Depending on how I was feeling, sometimes I would just scream and let out whatever troubles that were within. Other times, I would lay down and gaze at the sky until the stars came out. As an adult, I have made it a point to have my safe space near a body of water – preferably some type of river stream. I am absorbing my environment and often times my mind is clear, my heart rate is slowed, and I am able to focus on my breathing and the therapeutic sounds of the stream. In my safe space, I am free of worry, task, and the troubles of life – just the way it ought to be be in our safe space. I have a deep appreciation for my safe place. Without it I feel like I am continuously carrying the weight of the world, work, family, and friends on my back. I make time to escape and be idle in my safe place.. It helps me remain engaged when it is time to come back to reality. Where is your safe place? Have you unintentionally created one? Don't wait until you have time to release, make time. We don't want to wait until we are completed, weighted by the world, to start our healing process. Run off to your safe space, and when you get there continue to fuel your being so you can enjoy your ride without the worries of" burning out".

"If you have no idea of who you are, your *boundaries* will tell you. Boundaries show you where you end and *someone else begins*."

SET BOUNDARIES

*B*oundaries are so important in our pursuits to maintain a healthy lifestyle and healthy relationships. Boundary building isn't relatively new, it's just not a skill that has been taught or as talked about as it should be. We usually learn how to set boundaries from our own experiences or through the lens of other people's experiences. Having boundaries means that we are aware of our limits, and we are making others aware also. I once was a person without many boundaries at all. So in order for me to do so, I had to actually give myself permission. I was fearful; I had self doubt and guilt because I wasn't sure what my current social circle might say about these new found boundaries. I knew it required me to speak up and say no to certain things, but self-care was becoming a priority for me so I was willing to do whatever was required. What I learned is that I had to start small. Coming from no boundaries at all, I had to make boundaries that weren't so threatening to me and incrementally build to more challenging boundaries. I was a student athlete in college. Everything about my atmosphere outside of sports was more like a celebration. People were just genuinely happy to be in college and in the presence of others, and it usually involved alcohol. I had my fare share of indulging. I never abused it, but it started to become a distraction and that's where I knew I needed to set boundaries. I wanted to hold myself to a higher standard. My body wasn't recovering efficiently enough to take on college, an athletic career, and parties. I still went to social events, but I started limiting myself to a glass of wine every other week. Then it came down to one drink a month. Of course there were people who didn't agree with my limitations and didn't like hanging out with me as often, but what I have come to realize is that setting boundaries is a critical skill set necessary for growth. One thing I know about growth is that you win some and lose some – lose possessions, people, and time. If anything or anyone tries to alter the limitations I set to grow, I just knew they have to go. Be assertive with your boundaries, stick to it, and don't feel guilt ridden for doing so.

"Compliments are *gifts.* Receive graciously and simply say *thank you.*"

ACCEPT YOUR COMPLIMENTS

I have had troubles in the past recognizing compliments. Not only have I had trouble recognizing compliments, but when I do it is even more mind boggling for me to accept it – and not deflect, reject, or negate the nice things that are being said about me. For example, I could get a compliment on my makeup and point out the fact that I have acne. What does my response truly say about me? I'm sending a message that I am self conscious and not in a great mental standing to receive a compliment. Can you think of a time when you have been in a similar situation? When we do this, we are dulling down the compliment for our comfort. We are saying we think that the opinion of the person giving the compliment is flawed. Let's gear our energy towards acceptance. Don't be afraid to look that compliment giver in the eye and straight up say "thank you". They don't have to say nice things about us at all, but here they are, right in front of us, showering us with sweet words – connect with them. We have to remember to say "thank you". If we don't have anything positive to say following that "thank you", then just leave it at… "thank you". You don't have to explain anything. After these words of advice, if someone were to come up to me again and say "I really like your makeup today", I might respond "thank you, I switched to brighter colors on my eye shadow" or simply leave it at "thank you". Give compliments and be conscious of the responses you may get, but also put today's advice into action the next time you receive a compliment. Now you are geared to accept!

"The richest man with *bad health* will never be rich *in spirit.*"

HEALTH IS WEALTH

Over the years, I've been surprised at the amount of people I have met that do not schedule annual doctor visits and check ups because they are afraid of what they might hear or the results they might get. I am also one of those people. Health is the core of our being. It is what allows us to live happy lives and move without constraint. It's one of the greatest blessings in life. Think about how weary we can become being a person of broken health. If I get a common cold, I feel like the most dysfunctional person on earth, but then again I am somewhat dramatic. It's important to have a primary doctor to keep up with you and annually check beneath the surface of what's going on in your body to prevent the risk of any chronic diseases and promote our overall health. It's a part of taking initiative and being responsible for our temples. I know we have heard "it's better to not know than to know", but so many people end up feeling differently once they're deemed in irreversible illness that could have been prevented had they gotten a check up a lot earlier. Not only do it for yourself, but note that there are others out there including myself that love you and want to see you alive and well. One of my Queen mantras is "look good, feel good, do good".

"*Self-love* has very little do with how you feel about your outer self. It's about accepting everything about you and especially what is *within*."

MIRROR MIRROR ON THE WALL

*P*racticing self-love has been one of the most challenging things I've done because I didn't always love myself. It was hard facing myself in the mirror because the woman I was looking at didn't reflect the woman I had hoped to be. Did I get rid of the mirrors? No - I started loving the woman I was looking at into her best self. In those moments of practicing self love I did not feel narcissistic or full of myself, but I was trying to get in touch with me. I wanted to analyze my well being and my inner and outer happy parts. We practice self-love so we can overcome our ceiling beliefs and live a life truly reflective of happiness. Breathe, do good to yourself, and begin to research what you can do to provide yourself with all the self-love you desire. For starters, consume the food and water that help you live. You'd be surprised how changing dietary habits can affect our mood and skin! Stay active – push your beautiful body to occasionally do something vigorous and learn to love the skin that you are in. You have to stop comparing yourself to what society labels "the preferred". You have to stop comparing yourself to people you think have a lot more than you. Once we establish a genuine self-love, we are capable of getting to where we want to go.

"The best *love* is the kind that awakens the soul; that makes us want more. It starts a fire in our *soul* that cannot be put out."

YOU DESERVE LOVE

You are lovable and worthy of love. Once we believe that, it opens an entire new avenue for us to love and be loved. No matter how many times we've been hurt or hurt others, we deserve love. We need that love to cure the multitude of aches in our being – to prevent us from being hurt or hurting again. True love can do that. I think more times than not, what leaves us wondering if we deserve love is that love we failed to receive in certain situations or from a certain someone when we felt we needed it the most. We were left wondering, is it I? Do I not deserve love? Am I a person that cannot be loved? We have been put in situations with people who don't mind using us. I have been used, abused, and thrown away. It made me believe I wasn't desirable or deserving, and that mindset lured people to me with intentions that were not in my best interest. See, there's a song that only my heart sings and only a few will be able to dance to. Wait for the things and people who truly vibe with the fluency and melody your heart sings. In order to reverse that pattern, I had to redefine what I thought of myself. I had to believe I was worthy of the love I so eagerly wanted. Opening our spirit to only know love, light, and positivity is a stepping stone in receiving the love you deserve. Understand that there is a need for love, and above all else that is what we want and need - to be loved. To know that you deserve true love will embrace the freedom to enter a paradise for love that is beautiful to behold.

"Maybe you're not hard to *love*.
Maybe you're expecting love from
those less competent of *loving you*."

YOU ARE NOT HARD TO LOVE

*W*e have been with lovers who have left us raw and in question of ourselves – in questions of our hearts. We have allowed them to paint us as "hard to love", "overly emotional", or of a person requiring "too much". We have to keep in mind that more times than not, these type of statements are coming from those who do not really know how to adequately love. These are the people who do not love in the same capacity as we love. A new love can be overwhelming to someone who hasn't felt something so intense and pure. You are not hard to love, and the last person to make you believe such things isn't the only person you'll love in this life-time.That's right, there is someone out there specifically put together for you. This person will be able to receive and reciprocate the love that you give to them. The only hard thing about love is loving someone who doesn't want to be loved or doesn't know how to affectionately give that love back. I've loved and failed. I feel like I have loved and lost, but one thing I've learned from all of my romantic mishaps is that I am enough. Your love is enough, you are enough, and the love you so freely give will be returned to you in due time. Do not settle. Do not dwell. Do not dull. You are not hard to love.

"A life without *love* is like a sunless garden when the flowers are trying to *bloom* or are already dead."

LOVE MORE

Does is it need to be a specific holiday for you to extend love? Everyday we are awakened is a day that we can receive and give love in all the ways that we know.. I lost my grandpa to a very rare and progressive disease. I had gotten a call three weeks earlier saying that he was being transferred to the intensive care unit because he would not make it through the night. I instantly broke down and started praying for God to allow him to live a couple more days so that I could make it down and have one last moment with him. I remembered all the times he had wished for me to come spend time with him, but I was so held up with school and work I rarely made it. It just made me think about how much I wish I would have extended that love and appreciation for him more regularly because I know I wasn't doing it enough. We never really feel that need to show someone how much we truly love and care about them until it's too late. Thankfully, I had made it down in time to spend what was his last weekend. His spirit was so radiant, and he was so happy. That was exactly how I wanted to remember him. I was able tell him how much I loved him one last time, and I wished I could have done it more often and a lot sooner. Make today about extending your love and appreciation to your loved one, and being mindful that every waking moment is a day to give love. Let us not wait until it's too late to let somebody know how much we truly care.

"In silence you hear *life*. Be present, not just thinking about what will *happen next*."

SILENCE IS GOLDEN

*S*ometimes we get distracted by the clutter, chaos, and noise that surround us. We block out our voice of reason in an attempt to silence all of the noise present in our lives. Clear your mind, focus on your faith, focus on the possibilities, but shift the focus away from your problems. It may seem as if it's not one thing, it's another but know that your solutions and victories are within reach. Noise can be like quick sand that slowly sinks us in until we have minimal or no mobility. We have to get out of that quicksand, clean house, and silence the noise. This is probably easier said than done, but empty your mind. I am very concerned when I am not able to be present in the place of my own thoughts. When the noise of the world is louder than my intuition and voice of reason, I know I need to silence my environment and recenter myself. Silence is one of the most undervalued sources of great strength. In silence we have an opportunity to listen, reflect, and learn about what is going on in our hearts. Maya Angelou once stopped speaking for five years. In those five years, she read every book, and when she decided to speak, she had a lot to say and many ways in which to say it. She had felt saved from her difficult past in that muteness. She was able to draw triumphant out of her triumph in her silence. If the things in your atmosphere are a mirror image of what goes on in your mind, ask yourself "is my mind well ordered?" Then let us silence the overbearing parts and reorder our being.

"Connection is the *energy* that occurs between people when they are acknowledged and feel valued; when they can share without *judgment*."

CLOSE IN ON CONNECTION

*T*he need for people to connect and feel connected is unexplainably deeply rooted, but undoubtedly evident. What does that mean? It means that wanting to be connected is vetted in our human makeup. Feeling connected to each other makes us happy; it increases longevity. It's not so much the status of our networks, but how well we are connected to the individuals who make up our social circle. There is a need to belong, and it may not make a difference who or what we belong to, as long as we belong to something - that is how pledged we are to connect. It is almost like we have a craving for connection, and that is quite acceptable. I like to think of our human nature to connect like the food we consume. We need it to stay alive and to feel lively. Whether we like to believe it or not, we function a lot better when we are connected. It has even been shown that humans are more likely to physically and mentally fall apart in isolation. We are built for social contact. Isolation can come with serious consequences. Standing alone plummeted in your thoughts can get scary. The last thing I ever wanted to do was go through difficult times by my lonesome. Closing in on connection is crucial for our health. As much as society wants to make it cool to be the "lone wolf", understand that wanting to connect or belong is a natural part of being a human. Fulfill your needs!

"A *sleeping* woman will have nothing
more than *dreams*."

THE DREAMER

As humans, we function from a nourishment system. This trifecta includes partaking in the needed amount of social activities, various food, and getting enough sleep. Sometimes we are put in situations where we have to sacrifice one for the other in the nourishment trifecta. The average human is required to get eight hours of sleep to feel fully rested. Six hours or less could equate to little or no sleep, but what are the repercussions for exceeding eight hours of sleep – for oversleeping? Along with health side effects including obesity, depression, anxiety, and heart risk, we are missing out on our chance to do something or be someone. Tupac hit the nail right on its head when he referenced that the only true reward a sleeping man gets is rest of course, but dreams. Then, when we awake, we are faced with the pains of reality because we didn't invest enough time into being awake and making it happen. I had a certain commitment in my life which included my being in bed by a certain time to get a certain amount of sleep and awake early enough to get my day started. I wasn't always committed because I'd stay up all night and sleep through the morning to finally awake feeling sluggish. Then, I started going to bed late and waking up early until I finally put myself on a schedule. It feels nice to rest, but it feels even worse waking up and knowing we aren't living to our fullest potential. I tell my friends all the time, "there are 24 hours in a day in which we can be doing so much". I am not complacent being the sleeping woman with only dreams. I am going to get up and get after it!

"Fill your life with *experiences*, not things; have more stories to tell, and *less to show*."

EXPERIENCE LIFE

Don't be so captivated by all of the nice things you see other people or your peers possessing. The true pleasure comes in the form of memories and experiences. Great memories are made up of blissful experiences. Those outweigh anything we could ever buy on this earth. When I graduated college and moved into my first home, I spent more time traveling than actually furnishing my home, and I never regretted it. At one point I only had a TV, couch, and a bed that sat on the floor in my entire home. Some people have a lot less! I was grateful. I was okay with that because I had traveled to at least six different states within months to explore different exhibits and cultures with the people I loved. That love and joy I felt through these experiences filled up all the missing spaces in my home. What I realized is that the material items will forever be that, but there is no for certain stamp on the time we have to make memories and share grand experiences with the people we love. So next time you have to make a decision between that 75" TV and the family vacation, choose the family vacation. Odds are you will probably end up replacing that TV with some later enhancement anyway, but the memories you share and the experiences you have will last a lifetime.

"Meeting your *needs* is your job, and it belongs to *no one* else."

MEET YOUR NEEDS

*W*hat is it going to take for you to start putting yourself first? Repay the favors and be there for yourself. After all, look at all that you do. You are your own source of unconditional love, and you never leave or fail to give life all that you have. If you're not doing those things, you're working on it. Give it some time. Just for a moment, take a break from trying to figure out what the world needs and ask yourself "what do I need?" What keeps you alive and going? The world and the people in it are in need of people like you. That means your needs matter so don't ignore them – meet them. There is no problem with having needs and wanting to have them met; everyone has needs. The only way your needs go unmet is when you deem them as not being worth the effort. Maybe you can go without it or maybe you'll forget about it – right? But, this takes a lot of mental and emotional effort and convincing on our end. Whereas, we could have just used that energy to meet our initial need. If your glass is anything less than full, fill it all the way up. That's your job, and it belongs to you!

"It's not the *load* that breaks you down, it's how you decide to *carry it*."

PACK LIGHT

I remember being a teenager in high school, playing sports, and trying to manage my grades. At the same time, I remember trying to have a childhood, but that was shorted by the endless responsibility I took on when my mother became ill . I remember being in college, playing basketball, managing my grades, and trying to involve myself in campus activities along with the community. I remember trying to maintain certain relationships and outgrowing others. I remember giving people my last who wouldn't even give me the time of day .At one point, all of these events weighed heavily on my heart, and they eventually weighed me down physically. These situations didn't necessarily break me, but it was the way I decided to handle the things that hurt me the most. My neighbor told me "life is 10% what happens to you and 90% how you deal with it." That couldn't have been a more accurate translation of today's quote. If I would have asked for help and been more transparent about the things I was going through, maybe I would have gotten a fair shot at my childhood. If I would have been more organized, kept up with school, sports, and extracurricular activities, my academic career would've been a breeze. I probably would've enjoyed it even more! It's not the load of life that weighs us down; it's how we chose to deal with it. The way we carry it can break us. Our happiness is not defined by the absence of problems; it's our ability or inability to deal with them. There are 24 hours in a day. That means we have plenty of time to really buckle down and determine where we need to be spending our time. The point is that it's not always a matter of working harder, but working smarter that allows us to move through life weightless.

"Every great *achiever* is inspired by a great mentor. Every great leader was once a *prodigy* of a great leader."

MENTORS MATTER

I was on a conference call today with some of our leadership. We started something at my job where individuals are paired with a mentor in the area. When we began the call, the woman who was speaking stated, "being a mentor matters just as much as being a mentee". Everyone needs a mentor even if you already are a mentor." I attribute a lot of my success to having mentors. Mentors pull stuff out of us that we had no idea is within. I have had several mentors. Some of us on different paths, but all of us in alignment and geared towards growing. Do you have a mentor? We often have conversations about goal setting and navigating through my personal and professional life. They are the best when you need an extra push or words of encouragement. In college, one of my mentors was Miriam. She's just a few years older than I am, but full of life, light, and so much wisdom. I mentioned this earlier, but I came to school isolated, and I thought my only niche would be basketball. I fell in the routine of school and practice and just wasn't getting much out of my college experience. Miriam didn't have to, but she took it upon herself to introduce me to extracurricular activities, pageants, community engagements, and even introduced me to God. She lit up a light in me that people could see and feel outwardly. She lit up a light in me that I didn't even know existed. Until this day, she is only one call away when I need to pray or need some advice. I advise you to get someone like that in your corner. Get a few mentors! Sometimes it takes good people to pull the great out of us, and that is why mentors matter.

"Great wisdom is knowing *yourself*."

GOALS WITHIN

When I think about internal goal setting, there are a couple things that come to mind. One, Internal goal setting is just as important as your life goals. Meaning, I know for sure we have goals encompassing what we want out of life, but we should also be making goals about what we want to happen within. I have gotten a chance to talk about goal setting for your life and creating a blueprint to get there, but what about the inside? How do you want to feel? What thoughts are you having about yourself? Let's work on that today. For me, my internal goals are peace, health, and ultimate comfort with who I am and my purpose in this world. We may have completely different internal goals, but it is important for you to know what yours are. Think about it. What we can concur internally will reflect outwardly, and it is then that we will feel a sense of freedom. Not every day do I feel at peace. I don't always make the best health decisions – especially when it comes to food! I find myself questioning my "why" sometimes, but I am still working at my goals one day at a time. So should you. Be gentle. If we spent as much time focusing on the internal matter as we do the outward stuff, we would feel limitless and as light as can be.

"Make more *moves* and less *announcements*."

PROTECT YOUR PLANTS

We have a habit of coming up with ideas and broadcasting it to the world before we even make a solid effort to solidify any details. I like to call this making premature announcements. Your thoughts are important, sometimes fragile, and sometimes delicate. We don't have to share anything until we are ready to do so. In the meantime nurture these brilliant ideas you have, build, and watch your plans blossom. In other words, write them down, develop them, and then share.. I understand the excitement behind being creative, but when we announce things prematurely we find ourselves working to curate other people's deadlines instead of working for the fulfillment of purposeful work. We find ourselves rushing instead of putting forth quality work. Moves are better made when they're done in silence. There was only a select few I had told I was writing a book. Simply because I was so attached to the idea of writing a book that if someone had anything negative or dulling to say about it, I knew I would be highly offended. The last thing we want to do is plant in shade where we will have little sun and minimum growth.

"You can't *heal* what you hide."

REVEAL

There is so much stuff I have within me that I have had no urgency to bring to surface. I wouldn't say that I have been necessarily hiding these unwarranted traumas, but I have certainly not been eager to bring them forth. You could say I am a hoarder of my feelings and life events - both good and bad. These things often compile within me until one day I burst, and everything is unintentionally revealed. It all comes pouring out like a fountain of feelings. Jay-z said something to the effect of "what we do not reveal, we cannot heal". It makes me think of all the times the wise elderly folks have told me tales of history repeating itself because people never fully understand the magnitude of the past and present timest. When we do not get to the core or roots of our pains, they remain. Let us bring what's inside out and really put an emphasis on our personal healing. We don't have to share it with anyone if we don't want to, but really be honest with yourself. I have found that by revealing to myself what is troubling me, I am able to heal and carry a lighter load on my journey. I can't promise that this revelation will be pretty, but I can promise you softer thoughts and a more at eased mind. What we reveal, we can heal.

"You have to nourish to *flourish*."

KEEP ON

*H*ealing is a lifetime of work. We don't stop healing ourselves because one day we suddenly feel better. Self love, assessment, and assembly have to eventually become a lifestyle. Like anything living, it has to be constantly tended to in order to survive. Flowers are a perfect example of this. A flower in the garden needs light just as much as it needs water. It needs moderations of fresher soil. Without these things, the flower is sure to live a short life or not evolve at all. The best way to preserve a flower when it has fully bloomed is to keep tending to it. Keep tending to it like you're still in the beginning stages trying to get it to grow. We are the flowers in this scenario; we are constantly in need of fuel to keep growing..Healing is ongoing, continuous, and forever. In order to make everyday a good day, we have to be dedicated to our daily regimens of self-love and care. Do not be satisfied with one good day, when there is an opportunity present to have a good life. Get your water. Get your Light. Keep tending to your flower. Keep on

"So many *years* of education yet nobody taught us how to love ourselves and why it's so *important*."

DEAR SELF

One of my favorite women to watch in action is Valencia D. Clay. This woman is an educator, artist, author, and advocate of so many. I watched her at an event she hosted where she encouraged all of the women to write love letters to themselves. It was one of the simplest exercises to do, but yet so brilliant. The women took a few minutes to write a letter to themselves, and then they read it out loudly to the rest of the group. Each woman who read sat in the middle of the circle while everyone around her listened. I started hearing women remind themselves that they are love; they are beautiful, and that they are also worth everything. These are necessary reminders I think we forget to tell ourselves. We are better able to instill these thoughts in our minds Some of us have been stuck in self criticism for years, and we have forgotten to love ourselves for all that we are and have been. Instead of focusing on if the glass is always half empty or half full, celebrate the fact that you have a glass. Celebrate the fact that even though you are not where you want to be, you are not where you once were. I challenge you to write a letter to yourself as a reminder that you are love, light, and restore your personal positive image of yourself. Store it somewhere and go back and reflect on what you had to say. Great transformation takes place internally. There is an enemy within that we have to hush. This is only the beginning to a forever romance with yourself.

"When you need *attention*,
try giving it to *yourself*."

SORRY IN ADVANCE

I have to take a break from work, the things I have to tend to, social media, friends, and even family sometimes just to focus on the care and self love I need. I tune out what's going on around me and tune in to my needs to figure out what exactly requires rebalancing. We all have done it, or we all really need to do it. Some may consider this "disappearing". Well yes, I disappear sometimes. Especially when I feel overwhelmed and overly anxious. I call for my calm in isolation and come back to the world when I am at ease and feel confident in functioning like I regularly do. Apologize to the world in advance because sometimes we just need to take a time out to self love, to care for ourselves, to regather. When we don't cater to our needs and avoid the care we require from ourselves, we start to exhaust those negative feelings onto others. The last thing we want to do is be of bad energy in other people's space. Be good to yourself so that you will be good for yourself and others. Apologize in advance for taking the time to regroup and replug, but let there be an understanding that you're coming back. You're coming back recharged, ready, and as your complete self. Put a pause on all that you are doing for others and do something for yourself. Charge your "sorry in advance" to self care!

"When you do things for your *soul*,
you *feel* a river moving through you.
That's *joy*."

PLEASE YOUR SOUL

I took on a project that reminded me of value and transformation. As I watched construction workers build more houses around mine, I noticed they were discarding a lot of materials they thought to be useless. I pleaded with them in hopes that they would give me a pallet board or two for free. They did. The man walked it right along the side of my house and set it down. Unknowing what would become of it, there was a bigger picture establishing in my spirit. Their trash would soon transform into my treasure. It set there for days in the sun and storm. After deliberate research, I came to the conclusion that out of all things I wanted an indoor herb garden. With a little elbow grease, something that was on the verge of being abandoned could be transformed into what I would consider innovative, applicable, and soul pleasing. My father came in for the week and helped me put it together. He didn't comment on how ridiculous of an idea it sounded. He just rode the wave and helped where he could. I didn't necessarily need the herb garden, but I felt it was good for my soul. Afterwards, I felt such a great rush of satisfaction. I realized I had been lost in routine and enjoying very little of it. Engage from time to time in the things that please your soul. Every morning I wake up to make a cup of tea, I go and pick lemon balm off my vine and my heart becomes full. Sometimes we get so wrapped up in priorities and bills that we forget about the simple, yet pleasing matter. Do more inspiring things for the soul!

"I stay *ready* so I don't have to *get* ready."

STAY READY

I was recently mentoring at a Grow Lead Inspire conference where a woman by the name of Krissalyn Love was teaching us about taking our lives from ordinary to extraordinary. Krissalyn had told us her passion was singing, but there was a time that she felt discouraged because of the amount of money it takes to actually be in a studio with someone mastering your music. Then she thought to herself, if anyone were to come up to me today willing to pay for me to make an album and I only had x amount of days to do it, would I be prepared? She ended up recording the music on her phone to the best of her ability. We never know when an opportunity will present itself; therefore, the last thing we want to be is anything but ready. I felt the same way about writing this book. Life was getting in the way, and I had put down my manuscript for a while because of funding. I knew that I didn't have all of the money together right then to publish it, there would be a day when I would. When that day came; I wanted to be ready. What is meant to be will be and when the time is right, those doors will be wide open for you. So don't let not having all of the resources and funding distract you from doing the groundwork. That will come in due time. Do your part to make sure that when the time does come, you are fully prepared.

"The greatest *gift* you can give the world is a *healthy* you."

HEALTHY YOU

ood health is one of the greatest blessings of all time. We tend to miss the value in health until sickness comes to remind us how truly valuable it is. Life can look cold with rain and grey skies to somebody with broken health. Being in good health is important because women of good health will be able to get after life without many physical or mental barriers in the way. We are able to dream properly and awaken in great physical shape to make those dreams a reality. We can get so caught up in work and the world that we forget to take care of our mind and body. We can't be so focused on our pursuits that we forfeit our health. Success will mean nothing without joy, peace, and self-love. It's difficult to get to the next level when you're sad or physically ill. Remember, our mind has to reach our destination way before our physical being does. Good health goes way beyond the physical. I suffered from severe depression in my teens. I didn't think I could do anything and wanted very little out of life because my mind wasn't right. I didn't have a full knowledge of who I was and the strengths I possessed. Although I was a little bit embarrassed, I sought out help from physicians and therapists to bring me back to a sound mind. That was the right thing to do. There's no shame in doing what it takes to restore a healthy you. Only when we are physically and mentally healthy, will we enjoy a healthy life. A healthy you make for a healthy life.

"Focus on where you're *going*,
acknowledge where you are, but never
forget where you *came* from."

CONNECT WITH YOUR CORE

Rising and growing are where we put a lot of our focus, but it's equally important to acknowledge and keep in mind where we've grown from. No matter how high life takes us, we can't let go of our roots. I am shamelessly from Richfield, Minnesota. That is my core and those are my roots. Being a former athlete, my trainer always told me "your core needs to be strong or everything else you're working on won't mean much". For example, I have a degree; I'm employed and making great strides as a philanthropist, but there are times when I experience self-doubt. I have thoughts of my not doing enough. My energy becomes less, and I get stuck in this fog. Everyone goes through it. My solution isn't to book a groupon trip and get out of here, but my solution is to go back home to my roots. My solution is to connect with my core. My parents no longer have my childhood home, but I will go visit that neighborhood. I'll sit at the park across the street and stare at the home I dreamed in for eighteen years. Those thoughts of doubt become less when I reconnect with the little girl who lived on Portland Avenue. I appreciate the stability in the home I have built, but I embrace the ever changing chaos I rose from. It makes me cry sometimes, but I don't feel pain- it's more of an empowering break through. It doesn't matter if you grew up in a trailer, projects, mansion, or foster home. The dreams you had in those days are what got you where you are now. Disconnecting from our core is a sure way to slow us down from rising, growing, and transcending into a better life.

3
Weathering the Storm

"It's *just* a bad day, a bad moment, or a bad time - it's never a *bad life*. We spend all of this time praying for an easy life, when we should be praying for the *strength* to endure our difficult times. We don't come out of storms as we once were. We come out *stronger*, wiser, and prepared to take on new challenges. Storms force trees to take deeper roots. When the storm passes, they *grow stronger and taller*."

"The process of *self-healing* is a privilege. Self-healing is not a superpower. Self-healing is a genuine process of the relationship between the *body and soul*"

HEALING IS A
PROCESS

For many of us, we know that healing is not something that happens for us overnight. When we experience mental or physical pain, it is understood that healing will take time. How much time? There is no definite answer for that, but one can take as much time as needed. Some of our physical wounds take a little less time to heal than our wounds of the mind, but the common factor is that it takes time. There is a process we must go through to overcome, regain power, and feel that sense of stability again. In the process of healing, it is hard to continue with our regular schedule at full capacity. Internally we feel like parts of our shining world have been shaded which is often a normal way to feel. There is no way to make what we are healing from disappear, but there is a way to feel firm in your standing again. When we identify what's bothering us, it puts us in a position to really get to the core issue. We have to choose to no longer allow the temporary pain of whatever we are going through to keep us from smiling, loving, and going on with our life. It may be hard to see it now, but there will come a day where the pain feels a little less and our hearts are more at ease.

"No matter how *bad* the roads get, life is a journey that must be *traveled*"

ENVIRONMENT VS DESTINATION

No matter who you are, where you are, who you come from, or where you come from you will always have a choice to rise. Your current environment and circumstance have nothing to do with your destination. It is all a part of the journey. You have to have bold faith in your journey. You have to start believing that when the odds are stacked against you, it is not the end, and you will be able to climb over that wall one day. Many of you know Oprah Gail Winfrey. She has had the highest ranked television program and been ranked the richest African American. She is considered to be one of the most influential women in the world. Oprah had to fight to get to where she is today. It wasn't out of luck or being in the right place at the right time. She had to make a decision to rise out of her environment in order to be successful. There were multiple times when Oprah could've caved in and let life get the best of her, but she wasn't satisfied. Before her success, she lived in a rural town in Mississippi. Oprah has also mentioned becoming a mother at the age of 14 after being molested; she lost her child in infancy. The list of tribulations in her life goes on. For those of you who are not produced in the utmost nurturing and supportive environments, please know that your current circumstances aren't reflective of what your life will look like for the rest of your existence. One day an opportunity will present itself and permit you to rise, and only you have the choice to make that initiative and create something beyond imaginable for yourself.

"If you want *clarity* in your purpose or deeper and more meaningful spiritual lives, *vulnerability* is the path."

VULNERABILITY IS VALUED

*V*ulnerability is, the quality or state of being exposed to the possibility of being attacked or harmed - either physically or mentally. Being vulnerable means being open to pain and pleasure. Vulnerability has recently become one of my strong traits because I am now complacent with who I am. That's what people fail to tell you. Being vulnerable is not about solely exhibiting all of your pretty and shiny parts, but about opening up the parts of you that you reject, deny, and are slow to expose to other people. Being vulnerable is a choice that we have to make – and that we should make. For me, most of my vulnerable experiences have been faced by default. My first real experience with vulnerability came in a past relationship. I was so in love and so comfortable. All I knew was how to give – give my whole self, give time, give money, and give anything I could. The lack of reciprocity made me feel rejected, and I wore that like a vest. All of my relations were altered by this feeling of rejection, and I became guarded and less willing to share me. The vulnerability I was once so opened to share was now brigaded with fear. I have figured out that there are times when the outcomes of situations have less to do with you and more to do with the person with whom you are involved. Being vulnerable has allowed me to make valuable connections with places and people. It helps me to be honest with myself and stay true to my authenticity. Society paints vulnerability as undesirable and threatening, but in reality, vulnerability is the water that empowers us to bloom in love and grow stronger.

"Every defeat, every *heartbreak*, every loss, contains its own seed - there grows the wisdom to do better the *next time*"

ALWAYS A LESSON, NEVER A LOSS

*T*here is no escaping the fact that we live and we learn. Every day we face different means of adversity, and when we don't garner our anticipated outcomes or rewards, we experience a sense of loss. The ironic thing about adversity is that we, as humans. seem to learn more from it than any other human experience. It leaves me to wonder – is it really a loss at all? If I were to blatantly come out and tell you that there is no such thing as losing in life, you would probably stop reading the book, but hear me out. The secret to a "winning" life is to take your shortcomings, failures, and losses as lessons. We are not to let our downfalls keep us from aiming for a higher purpose. If we go for something and we don't get the desired results, ask yourself "what did I learn from this?" What can we take away from that experience in order to be better prepared and ensured for success the next time? We have more control in changing ourselves than we do in changing certain situations. Let us vow today to never let our doubts or fears of losing hinder us from even trying. I remember interviewing for a job that I was repetitively told was way out my league, but that did not stop me from applying. I knew I would be more upset if I did not apply at all than applying and the employer going with a different candidate. Let us take the good in our shortcomings, learn from it, and try again. There is no loss at hand when there is a valuable lesson to be learned.

" *Life* is like a camera. Focus, capture what will be cherished memories , *develop the negatives*, and if things don't work out, turn the camera back on and *take another shot*."

REMEMBER THE GOOD TIMES

Memory is how we hold on to the things that we love forever. It is how we hold on to who we are and the things we could not imagine going without. When we think about good times, what comes to your mind? Is it a loved one? Is it a concert, sporting event, or other social event? Whatever it is, you were probably experiencing a pure moment of bliss. Have you ever noticed that it almost takes experiencing very bad times to really appreciate the good – or to know good at all? If something positive in my life has occurred, I am thankful for the experience. I am thankful for those with whom I was able to share those moments. I am appreciative that our paths have crossed. When I find myself reflecting on my life, I make a strong effort to put my happy memories first. We need not dwell in negative experiences for long, but instead put our attention into the positive aspects of the past and things to come. As difficult as it may be, no matter the happenings of then and now, try your best to remember why life is precious – why life is beautiful. The roads may have been tormenting and difficult, but today, I vow to remember the good times.

"There are people who would *love* to have your bad days. So appreciate what you *have*!"

IN EXCHANGE FOR YOUR BAD DAYS

We never really know how good we have it until we meet that one person who puts it into perspective for you. During the summer, there was an entire month where I felt like I let myself go. I wasn't enthused. I didn't have much desire to do anything. I was performing less at my job and letting my responsibilities pile up on one another. I had a meeting one day that changed my entire attitude. I had a meeting planned with a woman I had never met before. We hit it off from the beginning. We shared similar interests, and she started telling me about her mission trips she takes to Africa every summer. She even invited me to tag along with her and her church! She pulled out a stack of photos from the trip, and as I am skewing through them, I felt tears rolling down my face. I saw women and children who were barely clothed, had no shoes, and lived behind metal and dirt. What shocked me the most was that despite their circumstances, the photos revealed something totally different. These photos showed all the people smiling and bonded in arms. She had mentioned that there weren't a lot of opportunities for the people of the village she was in to have a steady income. People stand on the streets for hours and wait for someone to drive by with a task for them to do so they can make money to bring home to their families. It made me never want to complain about work or about life in general. These great people were so satisfied with the little they had. I know in a heartbeat they would exchange my bad days for their current conditions. After that conversation, I left feeling grateful and a little ashamed . I felt ashamed because what I consider as going through a lot becomes a reality when I see that there are others on different sides of the world who go through a lot worse.

"Discipline is doing the *hard stuff* that unlocks doors that were once *closed* on you."

SELF DISCIPLINE IS KEY

*S*elf- Discipline is a quality we spend eternity trying to procure and preserve. It deters and we often fall off due to the lack of motivation within us. One of my favorite life coaches, Angelo John Lewis suggested that we adjudge ourselves to having three sleeves. The three sleeves are the conscious self, the basic self, and the higher self. Think of your conscious and higher self as two people, small enough to fit over your shoulder, both trying to advise you to the best of their ability. The basic self is our true self in the flesh. The higher self is the optimistic self. The conscious self usually uses negative incitement to get the basic self to change. Our conscious self uses words like "STOP" or "DON'T DO THAT". This approach momentarily works until we eventually end up reverting. This cycle repeats itself. Our higher self in this self-discipline sleeve that is usually the self to paint the positive picture. Higher self is thinking about the greater longevity of our decision making. Strong visualizations of our complete self being an effervescent, healthy, alluring person. Those illustrations can move our basic self to permanently transition out of those undesirable behaviors. So when you find yourself attempting to discipline yourself, make sure it is in a more positive manner. When I was in college, I wasn't the most proactive about my time. I could tell myself "stop taking naps" or "don't get on the phone", and I would listen for a split second until I reverted and repeated the cycle. I had to see the bigger picture in incidences like this. When I get my homework done, I will be able to socialize, nap, and extend myself without limitation. If I continue to exercise, I will eventually see results that will display a confident and strong me. If I save a little more money and spend a little less, I will be able to pay off my debts. Discipline is one of the most salient stepping stools on our trek to enjoying the luxury of what it is we are working for. So the real undistinguished task is working with our imagination to create a more motivating picture.

"The way you *communicate* reveals everything about you. You'll wear your words for the rest of *your life*"

COMMUNICATION IS KEY

*C*ommunication is the tree that bares the fruits of our life, work, and relationships. Without effective communication, what we say can be misunderstood, misinterpreted, and diminish the lucidness of our initial message. We are constantly exchanging information between people in our face to face conversations and even virtually. It is an exchange in which we try to accurately articulate our thoughts and intentions. The lack of the ability to communicate will set us back not only in our careers, but in our relationships. We have to be as good at listening as we are at talking. Many times we lose the ones we care a great deal about because of the lack of communication. A lot of our triumphs in relationship can be cured with communication, but effectively communicating is not something all people know how to do. We have to hear to actually listen, instead of hearing to respond. Good communication starts with knowing what it is we want to say and why we want to say it. Listen and avoid interrupting when the other party is speaking. We wouldn't want to be cut off when we are speaking.. Communicate to reach an understanding or an agreement. It is always a good idea to come back to the purpose of the conversation. Have we reached a common ground or resolution? It is okay to agree to disagree. There is not always a certainty that our communication will be met with agreement, but as long as there is understanding and respect, we are more likely to have an effective exchange. Of course emotions tie into the fluidness of our conversation and things may get a little off track but always remember to bring the train of thought back to its purpose. Remember communication is listening just as much as it is talking.

"Let your mess be your *message*. Don't
let your trials get you down - let them
inspire someone else."

YOUR MESS HAS A MESSAGE

Rest if you must, but don't you quit. Not to say what you're going through isn't already hard enough, but there is someone out there going through the same thing or even worse. Guess what? They're watching you. They are looking up to you to see how you will get out of it and probably even praying that you do! You are the necessary encouragement in someone else's life right now.. So whatever mess you are going through, major or minor, know that it shall pass, and that in the end you have a message. Your mess has a message. For years depression took over me until I finally made a decision to get on top of it. It was no secret, I was in therapy. For a moment, I was complacent with waking up everyday and feeling useless and hopeless. I thought plenty of teenage girls experience depression so it can't be out of the norm for me, but how many young girls actually make it out? I didn't want to be entrapped in those feelings of worthlessness forever. I sought out the right help, restored my faith, and forced myself to get up and get active. Eventually life became better for me, and the best part of it was when a younger woman came to me and said "I've watched you from then until now, and the way you have turned your life around has been very inspiring. I want to say thank you." At that moment, I was no longer doing it just for me. I was overcoming for the girls just like me in similar or dissimilar situations who at one point wanted to give up. There is a light at the end of every tunnel whether we like to believe it or not. There are people watching how we navigate through that tunnel in hopes that we will lead the way for them.

"Storms force the *trees* to take *deeper* roots."

LOVE YOUR LOWS

I used to ask anyone that would listen to me "why"? Why have I gone through such things? Why do I continue to go through such things? Why me? The real question is "why not me"? The lows in my life have made me who I am today. I wouldn't be the woman that I am without them. When I open up to others about the trials and tribulations I've experienced, I tell them that I am glad it happened to me. It forced me grow. It broke me, but the repair was beautiful. It reminds me of Kintsugi. It is an ancient art meaning "to repair with gold". When pottery pieces were broken, they would seal the broken pieces back together with gold. The Japanese believed that the piece is more beautiful for having been broken – just like us. We may go through some tough times, but nonetheless we will grow through it. We will come out of the pits stronger than before and ready to take on the world. Every struggle in my life has molded me into a better person. I am thankful for the hard times, and you will be too – for one day you will be able to see that it has only made you stronger. Whom do you want to be on the other side of pain? The struggles of our life are the greatest blessings in disguise. They often lead to the greatest moments in life. So we must not only love our lows, but we must remember to love ourselves in the midst of our lows.

"*High thoughts* must have high language followed by strong *conviction*."

SPEAK THE LANGUAGE

On average, human beings think over 60,000 thoughts a day. While impossible to monitor all 60,000, pay attention to the thoughts you give a voice. A good way to track for a healthy attitude is to talk about your blessings more than you talk about your burdens. I know… easier said than done, right? At times, the pain that follows our burdens seem unbearable. It's in our face and we can't help but to acknowledge it. We communicate through our words and bodily gestures. Our thoughts give us feelings that help us articulate what should be the language of our souls. However, it is never the words alone that affect us. Words are just words depending on how we use and associate them.. Our language embodies our attention and has the ability to color our lives and the lives of those around us. If you want to live in color, it is imperative to speak the language. Speak positively no matter what. We fight our inner demons daily, trying our absolute hardest to quiet our bad thoughts. Your words are powerful. Open your body and release what is dark so that you have more room for the light. Speaking the right language increases your joy. No matter how troubled the waters may be, finding the good in the rifts is one of the most wholesome things you can do. Practice positive self-talk. When you go on about your day, be conscious of the things you are saying. Find the aspects of your life that have undeniable light. The positive happenings in your life deserve a voice – give them one.

"Little things affect little *minds*."

FRAME IT

*F*rame your life with the "will it matter in five years" rule. When something happens that upsets you, pause for a moment, and ask yourself just that. Most of the time the answer is surely no. We give ourselves way too many things to worry about. Take a step back and look at what is troubling you with a wider lens. It helps us realize that some things just don't matter as much as we make them out to. A couple years ago, I had a hard time keeping things in perspective. I felt like everything needed to be addressed. I allowed minor things to get under my skin. I would reach to help other people with their issues, but I wound up making them my own issues. It was unnecessary, chaotic, and above all things draining. I didn't have much energy for anything else. I had to check myself. Is it really worth it? Will it even matter in five years? Sometimes it wouldn't even matter tomorrow. In that instance of realization, we must let go. We must free ourselves from ego, chaos, and conflict because our framing mechanism is only fit for the bigger picture. The bigger picture is most of our trouble today will be forgotten tomorrow and definitely nonexistent in the next five years. Frame on! Keep focused on the bigger picture and let the little worries wash over you.

"It's the little things that make *happy* moments, not the grand events. You have to crawl in *joy* before you can walk."

FIND THE PLEASURE IN THE LITTLE THINGS

*H*ave you ever noticed how euphoric you feel when life hands you the little things? For example, clothes fresh out of the drier, running into every green light, a compliment from a stranger, finding money in your pockets, the leaves during the fall, mist during the hot summer days, or the winter glow after a long snow . There are so many little things in life that bring us joy. Sometimes without our even realizing it or acknowledging it. An effectual path to happiness is not always through major events occurring in our life. It isn't always something that we have planned out like birthdays, weddings, buying a home, or holidays. It is most often the small and unexpected pleasures in life that make us smile each day. Pay attention to the fine details in life or the little things so that you can build happier, more meaningful lives for yourself and others. Take the day to take your mind out of your agendas, technology, social media,and look around at the gift granted to you- earth, life. My evening jogs became much more meaningful once I absorbed my surroundings. Running the same course was so routine; I had minimal motivation to do it! That was until I started noticing the little things like the trees on my path were changing, the leaves were either falling or growing, things changed colors when the sun came out, there were distinct smells at different hours of the day. It was beautiful to me. I shifted my attention to the more detailed pieces of my jog that made it more pleasurable. Not every gift is wrapped in a bow; the euphoric moments of bliss are found in the little things. Keep a keen eye out for those little things.

"True *love* is rare, but true friendship is *rarer*."

HOW MANY OF US HAVE THEM?

Genuine friendship is hard to attain. When we have those friends who actually feel more like sisters, we should keep them close in order to love them ,to guard them, and have them guard us. Most of all, we need to water each other. It isn't always blood that places value on our ties to people. It isn't always time that dictates how close we are or should be to someone. My friends and I share each other's experiences. In some ways we can feel what the other one is going through without physically going through it. We don't always agree, but we share similar values. We are a testament to our individual growth, and we are cheerful to witness each new individual milestone.I would be lost without these people. That's why it is important to openly express gratitude with your friends while you can. It hurts to feel undervalued as a friend. It's a different kind of pain when you feel alone in the presence of someone for whom you truly care for. Sometimes we are naïve to the fact that we are undervaluing our friends. I will be the "cheesy" friend that sends letters, morning quotes, or calls at 5:00 AM just to say hello. Little gestures go a long way. What are you doing to show your friends that you truly appreciate them? Be grateful to your friends that make you feel whole and allow you to be your authentic self. We need friends for the good times just as much as we need them for the bad times. They are like gardeners who tend to us and allow our hearts to blossom.

"Time has a *wonderful* way of showing us what really *matters.*"

TIME WILL TELL

When we think about human nature, we are usually referring to particular characteristics including our ways of thinking, feeling, and acting – which we all do naturally. It's a natural instinct to feel happy when something positive occurs in our life. It is also a natural instinct to feel upset or even angry when events do not play out to our expecting, but remember – that is human nature. I'll be honest, there are times where I can be a little dramatic or overly exaggerated, but … human nature. Time is the one inevitable thing that we have a little less control over. I would like to think our humanistic ways of functioning and time have a lot to do with each other. It takes time to get to our desired destinations. It takes time to heal. It also takes time to show us the importance of people, placement, and possessions. Some things will become known in the course of time. I would like to start a new practice today. I would like to think twice about the things and people I let affect me for one simple reason – will it matter in a year? Heck, will it even matter in a week or the next day? My rule of thumb is if it's not going to matter in three years, then I will not even spend more than three minutes being upset about it. We need to be a little more mindful of what we actually consider to be "problems". I have found myself sulking and being upset about certain situations without really realizing that in those moments I spent unhappy, time was passing me by- life was passing me by. There is no way to verify the magnitude of our troubles without time, but in that time, as hard as it may be, be happy and at peace.

"There are no *ugly* women,
only *lazy* ones."

LAZINESS IS DEADLY

*T*here are a number of reasons our dreams may never come true. One reason is because we spend so much time in the planning stages and never get to the "doing". Another reason is because some of us never try. Lastly, laziness – pure laziness. I admit, I have my days where laziness takes over me, but most times I make it a habit to assure all of my work is done. You can be sure I will be a lazy girl then, because I deserve it! I feel like laziness eats away common sense in the brain. Lazy people hate to be called lazy, but have no problem being lazy. They sometimes consider us "serious" and "overly ambitious". It's probably in our best interest to stay away from those who have lagging tendencies. What we don't want to do is get the idea that lazy behavior is ever okay. It could translate into stagnancy. One of my childhood friends once told me "you're too serious and you don't spend enough time being a kid. You're going to miss out on a lot." I think I was in or entering high school. I had fun! Probably not as much fun as sher, but I still had fun. I was on a mission to graduate and get on with my life. Needless to say, the childhood friend is still there. Things that grow never stay the same or in one place. Which one are you? Are you the lazy or "overly active" friend in this scenario? Remember that the only thing that comes to a sleeping or stagnant woman is a dream.

"If we were *meant* to stay in one place,
we would have roots instead of *feet*."

FEET NOT ROOTS

I grew up in a small town in Minnesota. For most of my life, I had loved it so much that I couldn't imagine myself living anywhere else. When I look back, I have met some amazing individuals with great potential to do just about anything they sought out to do. The strange thing is, some of them aren't doing anything. Without even knowing it, we brigade ourselves in the confinements of comfort. We stick to what we are familiar with because it is safe, but it doesn't give us much opportunity to grow. It doesn't give us much space to know ourselves and know the world. When I graduated from high school, I moved to North Dakota for school, and then moved again to North Carolina. It might sound unordinary and unstable, but I believe I was my best self in North Carolina. Traveling and relocating demand so much out of us. I am constantly becoming a better version of myself. To move away from what I am familiar with required me to take risks, get over fears, meet new people, and set goals for myself. I was stretched to my limits and full of life from all of the relocating I was doing. If I had to do it all over again, I would. I encourage you to put deep thought into where you are now and where you would like to be. Will your current environment bring you to your calling or capture you in its comfort? I now spend most of my professional life in Kentucky where I am still learning and equally as happy. Just because we are put in one place does not mean we cannot grow in another. We have feet, not roots.

"It is in the *small* things that great
strength lies - be *faithful*"

FAITHFUL

*A*re you pleased with where you are right now? In my personal experience, there have been times when I have set out to do things and have left them on the back burner. These little things accumulate over time and set undone. I wasn't being faithful in the small thing;, I didn't feel proactive. As a result, it left me feeling empty, overwhelmed, and a little stressed out. Can you relate? One of my favorite scriptures is Luke 16:10. It reads "whoever can be trusted with very little can also be trusted with much, and whoever is dishonest with very little will also be dishonest with much." That resonated with me in so many different ways. If I wanted the life I had imagined, I needed to become faithful in the little things. Faithfulness in the smaller of task speaks loudly to how you will be able to handle and operate within the lines of much larger opportunities. There is a sense of entitlement that lingers within us. "I deserve this… that." We find ourselves on a career path, but we need to be more concerned with the focus of our character. Are we disciplined enough? When we are prompted with very little and succeed, it will prepare us for the greater gift ahead.

"*Self-forgiveness* detoxes the poison
and the pains of your *past*."

DETOX

I called a friend a couple of days ago because I had noticed she'd been absent on social media for some time. She began to tell me about how free and unburdened she was feeling all because she was detoxing. I thought well, what the heck? What kind of detox is this? Apparently she let go of social media, limited her time on the phone, cut out sexual engagements, and increased her physical activity. I immediately commended her for her discipline. Some of the things we are most indulged in have a mysterious way of distracting us, and sometimes we don't even know it. I know that I am a clear victim of phone use and social media. I think I spend way too much time on both when I can be doing something more productive and less draining – yes, draining. When we are constantly plugged into items that subconsciously steer our energy, it gets draining. Social sites are one of the main contenders in that because of the clear controversy on our timelines almost every day. Is there anything distracting you, or do you feel like you may just need a break? It's a wise decision to fall back and detox or unplug every once in awhile. We come back feeling level with a clear mind and a body in full alignment – ready to get back to the grind.

"Knowledge is *power*.
Information *elevates* us."

KNOWLEDGE IS POWER

*E*ducating ourselves is a way of opening hidden realms in the mind. It gives us the power to choose wisely, come up with perspicacious thoughts, and ameliorate our lives. The more we know, the more valuable and resourceful we can be. Learning has been a pleasure. I try to learn something new everyday because all of this free education is nothing short of a gift. The only way to free my mind from little thoughts is to explore the unknown. It gives me perspective and an opportunity to see the true value of being alive. There is so much value placed on our physical possessions, and often we fail to realize that those things don't last forever. Those possessions could be here today and gone tomorrow. No matter what happens in our life, knowledge is something that can never be taken away from us. If we lost it all today, we would still have the power of knowledge to pick it all back up again. Dig into every book, digital source, or tap in to your elders to unearth your unknown. School was only a piece of the puzzle, but curiosity and personal research led me on the path to success. Reach the sources and connect to the unlimited power. No one can stop a woman with a will to learn.

"Fear is often *stimulated* by the loss of control. However, loss of control is the prerequisite for *change*."

LOSE CONTROL

*L*ife becomes a whole lot easier when we give up the need to be in control. If we avoid the need to necessarily make everything happen, we can let the universe take its course.. Quite honestly, I suck at this. I'm a perfectionist, a control freak, and I like things to go my way. My analytical nature brings me to plan, prepare, and prevent. My need for control stems from the attachment of various outcomes. I control out of fear. If I am in control, I am certain it will turn out this way – wrong! I have better luck when I trust that I will be okay no matter what. Have faith! We don't need to micromanage the universe. Lose control. It will open us up to endless possibilities that aren't as apparent with our sight on one "right" path. The crazy thing is the more I tried to control my circumstances, the less in control I felt. Over obsessing in the details just landed me in my own way. Always being in control doesn't allow us to learn the ropes of life. Controlling the uncontrollable blinds us from life's truth. Surrender – open up your arms and exhale all desires to be in control. Release the tension and feel the calm. It will allow you to see the bigger picture. When the time comes for us to blossom and evolve, we have to solely depend on the universe for the light and nourishment. We have to let go. Whatever we lose in lack of control only makes room for something better.

"I'm just *happy* that the thorns have *roses.*"

MUTE THE REALIST

I have been jokingly criticized as the tree hugging, save the world kind of friend, in almost every social circle in which I've been a part.. I am without a doubt the annoyingly positive and optimistic friend. At this point, I would like to consider it a gift in that I can find the good in the bad and the opportunity in the dust. "Reality" is a word sometimes transcribed with reason, but most times delivered by people with limited vision. Reality infects the little mind and has a way of disempowering our dreams. When I expressed some of my pursuits with someone close to me, I imagined a response like anything but the one I received. I told her "I'm working on writing a book, launching a website, and vlogging the creative process on YouTube." She looked at me as if I were crazy. Her look was her way of saying my priorities were beneath me. She simply responded "where the hell did this come from? What possessed you to do this?" I thought to myself "why not?" I was so close to caving in and believing that she was telling my truth, but she wasn't. My dreams were big, but attainable. In that instance, I had to remind myself that all of my desires were in reach as long as I continue to put effort behind them. I had to mute her! Not only will I charge you to hang around people that will reassure you that all things will come together, but be that person. It's so easy for you to limit yourself because it's not the picture reality paints, but paint your own picture. Mute anyone who gets in the way of your creative process, and then pass the brushes off to someone else to help them paint theirs.

"*Direction* is so much more important than speed. Many are going nowhere *fast*."

DIRECTION OVER SPEED

*T*he whole world is in a rush. Direction is far more important than speed. It's not always about how fast we are going, but where we are going and how we are tracking the things that matter the most. Many people are going nowhere fast – substituting productivity with busy. Although life is uncertain, and we aren't aware of our days, we are not in a race. It's a journey. A journey unique to all of us. Society would have us feel that speed is another one of those illusions that prod us to keep up with others. I would never enroll myself in a marathon without any knowledge of the finish line. One, I hate running. Two, where the heck am I going? My mind must arrive in the place I seek to go before my life does. Direction is key. We have to know what we want out of life and where we are going to get there. Step by step, you will get there. Resist the urge to hurry there – wherever you may be going. It's unsettling. Peace of mind must precede the peace in our lives. Peace and pleasure come from actually taking the time to smell the roses along the way. Peace is imperative in handling the intricate pieces of our journey with love. Everything we do lingers a sweet aroma, and we should take it all in and enjoy the fragrance.

"When you *compete* with a person, you're only competing to their standards and level of *competency*. If you compete with yourself, there is no limitation to how competent you can be or *become*."

YOU VS. YOU

*L*ately I started beating the sun to its day. I wake up every morning to face myself in the mirror. Of course I see me, but much deeper than the eye meets – I see my competition. It's easy to compare yourself with others. Especially since we are bombarded with images of other fabulous women on a daily basis. Life can be seen as a competition, but it is certainly not a race against anyone else. We are all competitive in our own right, but the real match is you versus you. When you open your eyes every morning, are you a better woman than you were yesterday, last month, or even last year? There is an old saying that suggest "if you judge a fish by its ability to climb a tree, it will its whole life believe that it's stupid." When you focus on your own magic and capabilities, the goal should always be to get better … to be better. When you compete with yourself, you aren't lured into someone else's metrics and values. You can only measure your success by evaluating yourself. Unknown competition has always been strange to me. We often go hard to be better than someone who doesn't even know we exist. On top of that, we barely know them! If you must compete, make sure it's against you. You are the only one in this world who knows you best and knows what it takes to be your best self.

"To have *faith* is to trust yourself to the water. When you swim, you don't grab hold of the *water*. If you do, you will sink and drown. Instead you relax, and *float*."

WALK OF FAITH

*D*arkness comes in many forms. It can come in bad thoughts, a failed driving test, breakups, acne, weight gain, job reallocations, and more. Darkness comes in many forms – all shapes, colors, and sizes. When we are living in these fallen times, it's hard to believe we will ever survive. It's hard to believe we will ever see the light, but we have to have faith. The walk of faith is the most challenging of adventures. The enemy will do its best during our walk to strike us and come at us like a strong wind or a cold rain. When we are deeply rooted in our faith, we remain steadfast, rooted and grounded, and we prevail. Faith is like film, better developed in the dark. Although we may not be able to see the victory, know that the storm will pass and victory will emerge. I was in my first career post college, and I had been with the company for about year. I was doing exceptionally well and thought I would be in it for the long hall. I received a call saying that there would be a downsizing and some of my counterparts were sure that I'd be affected. I could've worried; I could've cried. I could've put this book aside for the third time, but the best thing I ever did in this difficult time was not think about it. I didn't wonder, imagine, or obsess over all of the possible outcomes. I just let it be. I breathed and mustered up some faith that everything would work out for my good. Faith tells us not to get upset because change brings something much greater. Let your faith take its course to fulfill your destiny.

"We are often *punished* by our anger
and never for being *angry*."

LET THAT HURT GO

*T*here is a community within our society that feeds off pettiness, instigating, and drama. It's romanticized in our reality TV shows. "Trying" people has become "fun" or like a sport for some. Being slow to anger is a characteristic we all hopefully develop over time. We mistake anger as a stepping stone to power. I am generally slow to anger, but it takes effort. I'm still learning how not to let the opinions of others alter me. Although it gets to me, I realize the reward in rising above the fleeting passions. I have a clear understanding of who I am and what I say. I don't do anything with ill intent. No one can make me feel badly or steer me from who I am by using instigation and pettiness. I have noticed the intimidation that is cast on women when it comes to connecting and relating to one another. When forming new friends or acquaintances, we can be hesitant. I had to come around to the idea that sometimes the way people act has nothing to do with me, but it is truly a reflection of self.. People will cast their insecurities on you in a way that suggest that you should "dull down", say less, or be silent.. Do not comply, and do not become angry or feel less confident We must learn that we can't win by using the same techniques as the opposition. Self control helps us to realize that people are dealing with deeper issues. Anger is a cancer that eats upon the beholder. Self-control is the fruit of the spirit.

"You cannot change the *circumstances,* the seasons, or the wind, but you can *change* yourself. "

RECOGNIZE

*I*f you look up self-love in the dictionary, it will indicate that self-love is having regard for one's own well-being and happiness. We all have different ways to show that we love ourselves, but what they don't tell us is that self-love is more than basking in our light. Beyond filling yourself up with all the good stuff (which is necessary), self-love is also identifying where we go wrong, holding ourselves accountable, and making the necessary changes. Personal accountability is an ongoing commitment we make to ourselves. When we continue to identify how to be better, that means we are taking ownership and responsibility for our lives. We are taking action and removing the blocks that are in our way. Once upon a time, I was the queen of victims. I used to sulk on my throne of dysfunction and shortcomings. I wasn't fighting the fact that life just wasn't working out for me. My strength training coach in high school pulled me aside and told me "you have so much potential, but I don't even think you realize it. I need you to graduate and get out of here, but that means you start doing what you have to do in order to graduate! I know you can." I walked away from that conversation charged to be better – charged to get off of my sulking thrown and make what I could of myself in those trying times. I loved myself enough to recognize that I wasn't giving my all and that the world was turning even though I was still.

When bad things happen, it certainly isn't God punishing us or Satan "getting busy". Some of our hardships occur as a result of the choices we have made. You have to love yourself enough to right your wrongs.

4

Growing Through It

"*Growing* through it is a journey of discovery. It's about discovering what you need, what you feel, and how truly competent you are. You never go through anything without growing through it. It's like the *metamorphosis* evolution of the caterpillar - going through a series of molts, shedding its skin. The caterpillar radically *transforms*, eventually emerging as a gracious butterfly. A form only known because of the being's genetic determination to *grow* through it."

"A *rose* can never be a sunflower,
and a *sunflower* can never be a rose,
but neither the rose or sunflower
consider being any other flower beside
themselves."

BE YOUR OWN FLOWER

Society has a way of defining our means of beautiful, even if we don't ask them too. We constantly hear suggested criteria about our shape, size, and mannerisms – if we don't fit into their standards, we are deemed "less beautiful". The sad thing about it is that constant depictions on what we should be are everywhere. It's in the media, it's in your music, and it is now in your head. It took me a while, but I have grown to embrace my own type of beautiful. I don't always fit into social standards, and I do not think I am one they could put in a box, but I am unique and the defined details of my being make me who I am. Embrace that you are different and look for the good qualities that set you apart. We have to get out of the habit of comparing and contrast. We don't have to look like him or her to be beautiful. We are all beautiful in our own peculiar way. Saying it is not enough, but we really have to believe it. We have to build a thicker skin that no longer allows anyone or anything to define us. Any changes you wish to make on the inside or outside should solely come from your desire to change, not the influence of the world. Societal standards will no longer have an affect on us once we come to believe in our beauty and are comfortable being our own flower. Yes, a rose is beautiful, but I am a sunflower and rightfully so.

"Respect *yourself* enough to walk away from anything that no longer serves you or aids you in your *growth*."

R.E.S.P.E.C.T

*S*elf-respect is very important, and it's one of those things that you either have or don't. It is the navigation between how we treat ourselves and how we allow others to treat us. If I am being honest with you, I didn't always respect myself. I don't think that a lot of us actually take the time to sit down and deliberately think about the extent to which we self evaluate. I respect myself. Luckily, self-respect is not at all difficult to develop. A large part of constructing our self respect is defining our boundaries, habits, and what we will allow from others. I continuously ask myself what changes do I need to make to really face myself in the mirror and be happy with who I see? My answers are forever changing, but the good news is I have answers, and I am willing to adapt. Today, I respect myself enough to walk away from the things and people that no longer feed my spirit. I respect myself enough to walk away from spaces that undervalue me. I understand that attaching myself to such devaluing matters is detrimental to my growth, and I respect myself enough to walk away. Let us start treating our mind and body as we would the mind and body of someone we love. When you allow yourselves to fully gather this, you teach people how to treat you.. You will make necessary changes in how you obtain a certain respect when you view how you treat others and yourself and how others treat you and themselves.

"It takes making *mistakes* in order to do something truly *magical*"

YOU ARE NOT YOUR MISTAKES

Start treating your temple like a human instead of a machine. For us humans, making a mistake is almost inevitable. By understanding that you are human, you understand that making mistakes is all a part of the learning process in life. There is so much to life that must be processed by trial and error. There are certain situations that we must feel and fail in order to comprehend. It has been said that people actually learn more from their failures than from their successes. No matter how careful we may orchestrate our blueprints for our life, there will be mistakes, setbacks, and delays. Who we are as people is not defined by those, setbacks, delays, and mistakes. For a while I felt like people didn't actually know me until they knew about all of the mishaps and tribulations that have occurred thus far. I made it a point to make it other people's business. I would feel like I was bringing my complete and true self to any relationship when I would inform them of my mistakes and mishaps. It wasn't enough for me to speak so gloriously in regards to all of the good that I've put into the universe thus far. I was so shame-based and guilt-ridden that I didn't know any better. I stopped doing that because I no longer wanted to be defined by my mistakes. I no longer wanted to wear the substandard illustrations on my sleeves. My being radiates energy way bigger than any mistake I have ever made and so does yours. Those who let mistakes define others are dealing with something interpersonal that is completely out of our hands. None of us is perfect, but take a moment to look at yourself through the eyes of possibility. Think of it as such, as long as we have taken the opportunity to grow and learn from our mistakes, we are heading in the right direction. Let us stop mourning the parts of us that no longer exist.

"True *happiness* happens on the inside - it's in your thoughts. When your mind is at peace, you are *happy*. If your mind is at peace, but you have little to nothing in *possession,* you can still be happy. If you compensate with *physical matter,* but lack peace of mind, you'll be everything but *happy*"

PROTECT YOUR PEACE

*H*ow would you describe peace of mind? What does peace of mind mean to you? I've always wanted peace more than anything. Peace within myself, peace within my life, and peace with my career. For me, peace of mind has always meant the absence of anxiety, stress, and spiritual or physical discomfort. Peace of mind is an inner visual space I visit when I am experiencing serenity or a sense of calm over my being. In this space, my thoughts are quiet, and I am experiencing both freedom and happiness. Peacefulness is not a rarity at all. You often experience peace of mind without even knowing it - when you are in good company, enjoying the outdoors, exercising, reading your book, or listening to your favorite music. The difficulty appears when we are trying to either maintain or protect our peace. It is a very strenuous task sometimes. Especially when what is altering your peace is also the things you care a great deal about. I found myself laboriously attaching myself to things and people even when they didn't have my best interest. Think about that one friend, family member, or colleague who is so stuck in her ways. You try to advise and help help out of her troublesome situations, but nothing is changing. The only thing that remains consistent is her telling you all about her problems. It is important to note here that you cannot help anyone who does not want to help themselves. Be cautious of those people because you will end up carrying their burdens on your back - eventually weighing you down. Create a comfortable space between the things and people that dismantle your peace or better yet, let them be. Protect your peace. We humans cannot operate at our best with a fluttered head space, but we do have the choice to be very peculiar about who and what we allow in our space. Secure your temple. Your peace is more important than driving yourself "crazy" to understand why people function the way they do or why things have happened the way they did. Protect your peace. Let it go.

"Speed of *life* will kill more than it heals. Slow down to bloom like a *flower.*"

SLOW YOURSELF DOWN

When we rush, we don't get to thoroughly enjoy the flowers of life. Soon enough, life will pass us by before we have the opportunity to enjoy it. Our best work is not always put forward when we rush. We aren't being one hundred percent conscious of our surroundings which causes us to miss things. In my career,I keep up with many tedious tasks.. Early on in my career, I was so focused on getting things done that I would often make errors. Thank God for my manager because he literally has to be one of the most patient people I have met in my life. We need people like that in our corner, someone to say "we will get through this" and signal you to yield for a minute to get things done efficiently instead of in a hurry. I was missing out on the beauty of my career because of the pace in which I was operating. Working fast isn't always productive or labor-saving. There's no methodical logic to rushing besides the fact that if we get through it fast, it'll soon be done. But, where is the joy in that? Not only with our careers, but what do we get out of anything if we are rushing – rushing through love, school, relationships? What are we learning? What are we retaining from these experiences – probably very little to nothing. When we find our mind wondering to things we need to do or something that might happen, we have to gently remind ourselves to be present in the moment. Focus on what's going on in your current actions, environment, and with those around you. When I find myself speeding my way through and stressing out, I remember to pause, breathe. Breathe some more and really bring myself back to the present.

"What is meant for *you* is already yours or on its way - without force, stress, or *manipulation*."

STOP WATERING
DEAD PLANTS

I have a great deal of experience in trying to keep things that do not want to be kept – including people. Some of you may be able to relate to this experience of holding onto people despite the enthralling information and connection with that person that clearly communicates we would be much better off without them. For some reason we feel a need for their company. In my twenty three years, I have had multiple connections with partners, friends, family, and even work related acquaintances that have left me dry. What really got to me was the fact that I would repetitively give out chances and forgive, but some things were never really able to reciprocate on the other end. It hurts our feeling to feel alone in these relations. It hurts to feel like the only person trying or making efforts to keep the relation alive. At what point do we stop forcing theses relations and hurting ourselves? As we grow and figure out our own values, we build up a sort of knowledge that assesses our boundaries and decides which relationships we want to continue to invest our energy. We possess the power to let go of anything and anyone hindering us from excelling. Do you value yourself enough to say "enough is enough"? I remember telling someone "you are the most beautifully damaged person I know" and in that moment I knew in order for me to grow I had to stop watering them and instead water myself. Remember all relations require efforts from both parties. Personally, I want to invest in someone who's pouring into my cup as I am pouring into theirs. Moving forward and letting go is a pain, but forcing the relation sometimes takes away from your self worth and doing better by you. Choose you over anyone who has you questioning how you feel about yourself because you are enough. We have to let go of the few rich memories of these people and take them for who they are. They can no longer fit into my space because they are no longer helping me grow. We can no longer ache for what wasn't, but secure an appreciation for what it is. Our happiness, self-worth, and purpose are never about who is or isn't in our life. Understanding that is your power.

"The secret of *change* is to focus all of your energy on *building* the new instead of fighting the *old*."

CHANGE IS FOR CERTAIN

*A*djust, adapt, amend, modify, revise, refine. To make or become different involve all different variations of what it means to change. Change can feel great, bad, or uncomfortable. Things are always changing whether we like it or not. People come, they go, jobs end, we get promoted, the weather is suitable enough to swim in or ski. When positive change comes about, we have to start taking it in with grace. Whether you believe you deserve it or not. if you're questioning if you're prepared for that change, keep going and take what you can from it. If possible, explore other options before negative changes occur. Start planning alternatives on how you will bounce back. For example, hypothetically speaking, if you know your car is in need of an oil change and you're questioning how much further you can go without a technical dilemma , don't wait until the car gives out on you to tend to the issue. When we have an opportunity to do something about our situations before they actually occur, and we are deemed with the consequences, we have to start doing all that is possible! Change can be a good life experience just as much as it can be a negative one. "Go with the flow" is one of the most undefeated phrases of how to deal with life and all of the changes that can occur. If you find yourself constantly discombobulated by change, don't be afraid to ask for help from family, friends, or even support groups. Change is for certain, and it is the one thing we have the least control over, but there is always a way to adapt and come back to center. Let go of the constant need to be in control because most times we have the least control over change.

"When you allow *yourself* to be fully transparent and vulnerable, others will have the *courage* to do the same."

TREASURE MY TRANSPARENCY

*T*ransparency is the language that speaks openness, communication, and accountability. Transparency is operating in a way that is easy for others to be let in a world and see the colors we see – vividly. When you allow yourself to be transparent, you give raw emotions without any intention of dulling, trying to understand, or fixing them. There is nothing to hide when we are being transparent because in those moments, we are too busy being ourselves to even worry about the ridicule or the judgment. I've hidden behind masks that have robbed me of a happy and full life. A mask that hindered connections from people, places, and things. All because I wasn't being transparent with who I am or true to my authentic self because of the fear of rejection and not knowing if anyone would be able to relate. I wasn't the same person years ago as who I am today. My transparency is what I'd attribute to a lot of my success because it was through transparency that I was able to connect with others. It was through my openness that I was able to share my human experiences and actually get people to listen. Instead of hiding that, I decided to talk about it. There are people out there who share your same story – people who won't judge you and will help or follow you along your journey of growth. We won't be able to meet these gems until we open our" chest" and our hearts, and let them in.

"Thick skin is built from *humility* and self awareness. It is through knowing who you are that *protects* you from the people who do not."

THICK SKIN

What I mean by "thick skin" is that those stones they throw at us don't break our homes – they don't even leave a scratch. We know what we are made of. Do they? A decade ago, those stones would have broken me, but I have thick skin now. I know who I am and the words of those who do not no longer affect me. Ugly, broken, fat, slut, misguided, outspoken, aggressive, loud, lost – barely touch the surface of words they continuously try to bury us with, but like Dinos Christianopoulos said "they didn't know we were seeds." Seeds to emerge from deep roots and grow to be thick in skin and weather proof. Just being alive opens us to criticism, but acting in the public eye will dismantle an even bigger target on our backs. When we go high, we can be sure others will aim at us. It's not so much what anyone has to say about us anymore, but what we hear and what we allow to stick. The more we are able to identify who we are and who we are not, the greater our ability becomes to withstand the criticism. Growing up, I've realized most insults have nothing to do with me, but they have more to do with the person delivering them.

"If you're *lucky* enough to get a second chance at something, don't *waste* it."

REDO

We often spend our time overthinking, stressing, and over analyzing. It's not just u;, it is a human thing, and we all do it! We are all beautiful in our own specific way and even flawed in our own peculiar ways. The beautiful thing about our existence is that another chance to wake up means another chance at life. Everyday we open our eyes is a redo at life. We have the ability to start or discontinue whatever we please as long as we are alive to do it. Every waking minute that our body allows us to breathe and blood flows through our organs is a second chance to do something we wanted to do, should have done, or have never done before. We should be taking full advantage of the opportunity because life is never promised. Have you ever had conversations with elderly persons who wished they could go back in time? They wished to go back in time and make the most out of those moments when they were full of youth and physically able to handle all that life threw at them. We never know how long we have to fulfill our dreams or how long we will be privileged to be alive on this earth. All we know for certain is that we can seize the moments given to us while alive to do so, so take every living moment as a chance to start over, be better, and give life your best shot!.

"You may think the *grass* is greener on the other side, but if you take the time to water your own grass, it would be just as *green*."

MY GRASS IS GREEN

I used to find myself comparing my life to those that I considered already successful. It is kind of embarrassing to say, but I felt a little envious – motivated, but envious. I couldn't quite wrap my head around why I was working so darn hard and didn't have things to show for it like others did. I let the physical rewards of success drive me to think that I wasn't doing enough. One thing I have learned about my journey is that it is just that, MY journey. It is beautiful, flawed, and steady, but it is a journey specifically designed for me. I have a reason to believe that all of us on earth have an individual purpose along with a pre planned route. You may not think you are shining like the next person but understand you are shining in your own way. Our journeys may or may not be full of glitz and glamor, but as long as we have purpose and what we are doing is impactful in some way; we should be fulfilled. Live life like you, love like you, and continue to be your own type of beautiful. Focus on watering your own grass. Trust that everything that is destined to manifest from your hard work will make your grass green. There's no need to be envious of the next person getting it, because you are only looking at what they allow you to see. We don't know anything beyond that. We are no longer allow-ing our thoughts to ponder on "greener" because we are just fine with our grass being green. The greener it gets the more we focus on our own yard.

"Personal *accountability* requires mindfulness, acceptance, honesty, and courage to *correct* yourself."

I AM
ACCOUNTABLE

I am accountable. I haven't always been, but today I am. There's nothing easier than blaming someone else for the way that we feel or something that has happened. I am accountable for the love and energy I let in my life. I also take responsibility for the hate, betrayal, and deceit I let stay. Fool me once, shame on you. Right? We dismiss the warning signs and true colors the wrong doers show us the first time in hopes that they would strive to be what we hoped they could be. I like taking responsibility for my thoughts, feelings, and actions. At the end of the day, we all have a choice to feel what we feel, say what we think, and do what we do. Whatever we choose to do, we are held accountable for that whether it has a positive or negative impact. We possess the power and ability to detach ourselves from anything or anyone hindering us from the joy life brings. I have learned to love taking responsibility for my thoughts, actions, and emotions. I have learned to hold myself accountable for every waking move I make. Who better than me? Who better than you?

"You can't do a *good job*
if your job is all you *do*."

WHY SO SERIOUS

*I*f you knew today was your absolute day on earth, how would you reflect on your life? Did you live a good life? Was it filled with laughter, love, and smiles? Did you have fun? There has to come a day where we put down our Girl Boss hats and have a little fun. Life doesn't always have to be so serious and that is something I am still working on and constantly reminded of by my loved ones. I am a firm believer in working hard, but I also believe we women have to play equally hard. Balance! We have grown up in a world that tells us "work hard to be somebody". Without occasional fun, it limits our spark, our happiness, and our desires to do work or anything at all. Take some occasional time for you and indulge in the things that bring you laughter, joy, and peace. I like to think as work and play as two synonymous forces that cannot manifest without one another. Too much play does not substantiate for a substantial life, but just enough play will fuel you to maintain a healthy work-life balance. A healthy work-life balance means something different to everyone, but the compounding stress from everyday work will catch up to us unless we occasionally unplug and enjoy life. So, why so serious? Play as hard as you work and work as hard as you play. You will reap the same rewards if you follow that formula; the benefit will be sheer joy.

"Life is like a *marathon*, not a sprint."

TORTOISE VS HARE

I used to approach new task in my life with an "all or nothing" mindset and expect results on sight. I expected to become what I like to call either an instant or overnight success, but where is the reality in that? We all know that good things take time. We don't come out of the womb fully equipped to take on the rest of our lives; we have to grow first. That takes time. A small percentage of people are great spouses the day they get married. A large percentage take time to evolve into great spouses. We have to stop approaching our life as a sprint. We have to start putting logic into the pot of our aspirations. Understand that you can not give something your all at one time and instantly expect to be where you projected. We have to start being marathon runners in our life instead of sprinters. Like marathon runners, we have to train and condition ourselves. It's about becoming one and in tune with our body and spirit. This can apply to my future business owners, students, future home owners, parents, and just about anyone else. I, since high school, have had many aspirations about owning my own women empowerment organization. I understood there were many things I had to learn, plenty of connections I had to make, and a lot more credentials I needed to earn to obtain such a platform. In order to do that, I know it takes more than one book. It takes more than one seminar. It takes time! There will be times where we may meet defeat and stumble, but we will not fail as long as we continue to get back up and complete the race.

"Nature feels no need to *hurry*, yet *everything* is accomplished."

PUT A COMMA

When we constantly find ourselves on the go, it may be time to put the comma on our path and pause for a minute. Do some self reflection, take inventory, and find out if we are emotionally and physically taking care of ourselves. Being "busy" doesn't always mean we are being productive. I have found myself trying to do 48 hours worth of work in 24. It makes me second guess if it is even quality that I am bringing forth. During this yielding moment in reflection, think about how blessed you are. Can you think of something? Breathe into your hand, there's one – breath. You're alive. If you're reading this, you have site. We have favor and we don't even realize it because we are too busy being... busy. The moment we start acknowledging that life is a blessing, I promise you, it will start to feel like one. All the supernatural powers are working for us whether we see it, feel it, or believe it – they are working. Pause- It's not so much the world that we miss out on when we are always on go. We miss our sense of direction, our sense of purpose, and sometimes even our "why".

"*Success* isn't about where you are, but about all that you had to *endure* and *overcome* to get there."

OVERCOMING

*T*he sweetest revenge by far has been overcoming. Life for me has been about figuring myself out and figuring out how to get through each day. Some days are harder than others. There are times when we are judged by our performance and achievements. Those people who judge us determine our fate and don't often consider outlying issues because they already have their minds made up about who we are and how much we will get out of life. Growing up, I dealt with depression, anorexia, anxiety, and took on a great deal of responsibility when my mother felt ill. Instead of receiving help, I received judgement. "Bryann won't be much. She'll probably be stuck in Richfield for the rest of her life. She might not even make it to college." While that was what looked like the path I was treading, it's not the path I had envisioned for myself. Whether anyone believed it or not, I knew I was capable of more. So at that moment, it's truly up to you to prevail and live a life that sometimes you only see for yourself. There is so much to celebrate once you get there. Overcoming forces us to grow. It stretches us beyond our comfort and takes us to heights we've never been. So when the going gets tough, tune out all of the negative projections about your future. Only you are in control of your fate, and I hope you believe it is very possible to overcome.

"No *change* means no growth. No growth means no *life*."

THE BUTTERFLY EFFECT

*J*oday is about self realization. It is about understanding what you think is your purpose and coming to face with your current state of being. At this very moment, there are some parts of us that are not totally congruent with who or what we want to be in life. Whatever that may be could be troublesome or even hard to let go of, but we have to start looking at our ultimate callings. Like butterflies, we are all going through life cycles. Each stage is uniquely different, but the butterfly will only experience four different stages while we experience many. Butterflies start off as eggs entering the world. It takes about a week for them to transition into the little worm like caterpillars. It is in that stage where they are constantly fueling and feeding to prepare for their next stage. That next stage is the chrysalis. Not only is this the resting stage but also the growing phase. It is in these moments that the insect physically outgrows its current state. The caterpillar starts making executive decisions to meet its purpose. No longer will it feed off the leaves and shrubs, but it begins to sip sweet nectar from the blossoming flowers. What once was a caterpillar will no longer choose to crawl, but instead fly. This creature will see new heights never seen before, and the only way this will be possible is by shedding of old skin and habits. Butterflies don't reach the butterfly state until they shed from being a caterpillar and thinking like a caterpillar. It is only then that we too are able to fly.

"There is no *shame* in having a
perfectly normal human *experience*."

NO NEED TO PERFORM

One of our biggest disconnects with connecting to others is our ability to be human. In being human, we know that we make mistakes, we cry, and we get back up again. In the midst of all that, some of us can relate to what I like to call "performing". Performing happens when we turn our super human on and hide our disasters with our egos. Performing is battling demons on the inside but doing everything we can to prevent that from being reflective on the outside. Performing is losing your job but not once speaking of it to your family and friends. It is when we face something that could potentially break us but pretending to be okay. Are we ashamed to ask for help? Are we embarrassed to be any less than one hundred percent twenty four seven? Do we not believe that for everyone on earth it will not always be rainbows and sunshine because it isn't. I know there are bits and pieces throughout this book where I get a little vulnerable and elaborate about my life, and I did that for a reason. That was the only way I would've been able to connect with you all – through my life experiences. Performing to portray a perfect life is not only tiring, but it limits us. It limits us from our truth and the people and places with whom we can be connected. Creating an image to impress others or block us from pain tarnishes our intimacy and authenticity. It doesn't allow us to properly heal or move forward. We are all flawed pieces of perfection. There is no need to perform.

"It's not about *you*. It's about them.
It's about the *impact*."

IT'S NOT ALWAYS ABOUT YOU

*T*here was a challenge going around on social media where people were posting a regular photo of themselves along the side of their graduation photos from either high school or college. In the regular photo, they would caption it with all of the tribulations they had to overcome to get to the graduate photo. I partook in the challenge. I knew there would be some people who were offended. I knew there were people who wouldn't quite understand because, in my time of trouble, I didn't really open up about my life. They were only able to see the surface of things. So, in my regular photo I had captioned "2.5 high school GPA, severe depression and anxiety, unstable household, labeled lost cause and wild". I instantly got a lot of feedback from the post – both good and bad. Many people were pretty receptive to the post and showered me with thanks for sharing some of my story. One of my family members called and was trying to figure out what was so unstable about my life and if I had really believed I was a lost cause. The truth of the matter was that I did. Because of everything that I was going through, I fed so deeply into the naysayers that I forgot about my potential. I forgot about my dreams, and I allowed my circumstance at that time to pull me away from my purpose. The last comment I got regarding this post was that "it's not always about you". I couldn't agree more and that's exactly why I posted it. Not only do I think I was intentionally put through my hard times to be walking evidence to others, but I posted it because I wanted everyone to know that no matter what we are going through, whatever environment that we are in, it doesn't have to determine our destination. Sometimes our stories are to be told. Sometimes our stories say what the next person needs to hear or see in order to overcome.

"Learning without *thinking* gets you lost. Thinking without learning puts you in *danger*."

LEARN TO
UNLEARN

From the very first day we arrive in the world, we develop habits, thoughts, and ideas similar to the ones of our overseers. For example, people aren't born racist, that is a character trait one might develop or acquire from parents or other family members. I know that may be a bit much for an example, but it's true and even true in many other examples of such habits that are passed along. Sometimes we have to learn how to unlearn some of our bad behaviors from our developmental stages. These are the traits that have been influenced by others. One thing we have to believe is that it's possible to unlearn behaviors, thoughts, and ideas about all things and people. This all stems from an openness within us to do that. We have to be able to give up what we thought was right in order to really know our truth, the truth about others, and the truth about the universe. I always make it a habit to ensure that I am separating personal thoughts and feelings from the actuality of things. When we were younger, almost all of our educators had taught us that George Washington's teeth were made of wood. We never questioned it once because there is a certain trust we put in our teachers. Why would they deliver anything, but the truth? As we got older, we realized once wood is wet, it's useless. Wet wood deteriorates and becomes soggy. If he would have had wooden teeth as they said he did, he would have been in for a mighty infection. It is a myth that I have recently discovered at the age of 23, but I would have never known if I hadn't taken it upon myself to research and find the truth. The truth was even more disappointing when I found out from whom his teeth actually came.. You're probably confused and wondering why I chose that specific example. I chose it because that particular example lingers in my thoughts everyday. Everyday I am unlearning things I put certainty into. I'm allowing my curiosity to spread like pollen in hopes that the truth will rise. Learning is essential to prosperity, but you want to make sure the information you are taking in is factual so you are not later made the fool.

"Life is like riding a *bicycle*. You have to keep moving in order to find *balance*."

KEEP MOVING

I didn't really learn how to ride a bicycle until I was about nine years old, and I still suck at it this day. It makes me think about the difficulty in finding motivation to keep on when I encounter the hard stuff, but life is all about balance. I firmly believe that we have to experience hardships to fully know and appreciate the good. It not only keeps us grounded but level headed. If we find ourselves in a circumstance or environment for too long, it's time to go. It's time to move. We aren't really feeling life out if we are trying to do it stationary. There is only so much insight you can take in from one place. If I am spending entirely too much time on one thing, I know there is something else out there that's not getting enough of me. You have to keep moving. You have to find your balance. What balances you? For me, it's a combination of my family, my significant other, my career, and Christ. Each monument requires a different piece of me, or it requires me to be in a different space. Either way, I am always moving. I am always grounded. I am always aiming for balance, but definitely never stagnant. I have a friend who is an absolute girl boss and every time I turn around she is traveling. She is capable of picking up, going, and establishing new grounds so effortlessly. I admire that about her. When I asked her why she was always on the go, she said constantly moving has allowed her to keep her creative juices flowing. Being in new environments has enabled her to add new perspective and bring more value to her business. Once that well runs dry where you are, do not be afraid to keep moving in order to regain your flow.

"Decisions define *destiny*."

THE FROG THAT JUMPED

*H*ave you ever heard the parable about the frog in boiling hot water? The tale insists that the frog fell in a vessel of hot water. As the water grew in temperature, the frog had no desire to jump out. Instead, the frog adjusted its body temperature accordingly as the temperature grew. The water is boiling and the frog is no longer able to adjust his body temperature to manage the nature of the water. At this point, the frog tries to jump out of the vessel, but it does not have the strength due to all of the early adjusting.. Do we blame the hot water? Do we blame the frog? The frog couldn't make it out of the vessel due to its personal inability to decide when to jump. There are situations we will face in life, but there comes a time when we have to face it and take action – even if that means jumping out. Sometimes all we know is boiling water. We are so accustomed to those conditions that we don't realize how deadly it can be. In order to know when it is the appropriate time to jump out of the pits and into success, we have to have a full assessment of our surrounding and our strength. You are more than capable and qualified to make rational decisions. Decide what actions you need to take before it's too late.

"Being an *adult* isn't a matter of age. It's a matter of accountability and *responsibility*."

ADULTING IS...
DIFFERENT

What is adulting? Adulting can be a compilation of many things. Adulting is calling home a little less or not at all because at this point, you're independent and solely reliant on yourself to function in this world. We are paying bills, making our own meals, and most importantly making our own doctor appointments. How stressful right? The best advice I can give you on this one is to not rush to grow up. Enjoy your youth and appreciate the presence of your parents. Being an independent woman is extremely fulfilling and has its pros, but you will miss your minimal chores and waking up to pre cut waffles at your mom's house. When you're an adult, life is like one big chore. There's no siblings or parents to split your household duties with because you're now in charge of it all and then some. Another thing, do not expect perfection. Being an adult is everything but perfect. You will really have to feel your way through it, see what works, and find your groove. This takes time and on your first try it is likely you will fall down, but I encourage you to get back up – no matter what! It'll get better. Adulting is completely different, but life is progressive, and one day we have to face the music of being an adult.

"It's *important* to keep track of what you're doing and where you're *going*."

TAKING INVENTORY

Do you remember that workshop by Krissalyn Love I was telling you about? Let's do the "taking inventory" exercise she taught me. Get out something on which you can record the questions and your answers. What are you good at? What brings you joy? What can you make a profit doing? What can others depend on you for? When I answered these questions, I was surprised that all of my answers were in some way connected to one another. I found my gift. I could say that it reiterated what my purpose is. I like to serve and uplift others. When you do your inventory exercise, what picture will it paint of you? If by now, you don't have a clear understanding of your purpose, this will be helpful in figuring that out. Once you figure it out, I challenge you to use your gift for the next 30 days and work towards making it something. In these next 30 days, you cannot compare yourself to others you see using their gift, there are no "buts" or "what ifs", and you cannot stress about lack of resources or money. If it's meant to be and you give it your best, all of those things will come to you in due time. For now, take inventory (plant) and work at it consecutively. Watch as all of your hard work starts to manifest. I know you will see results (harvest)!

"Be *brave* enough to be your true *self*."

YOU ARE BRAVE

When I was a little girl, I used to think being brave meant jumping off the slide, falling into the turf, and getting extra points because I scraped my knee. Bravery was sitting in the very first cart of the log ride with my dad at the Mall of America, even though that's where I'd be splashed with the most water. As I grew, my definition of bravery has been greatly expanded. I realize that bravery is not always about putting myself in harms way or facing potential dangers, or proving myself. Being brave is more about stepping outside of our comfort zone. It's about having courage and having the ability to endure. Some of us are courageous everyday, and we don't even realize it. It takes courage to get out of bed everyday and face society. Bravery is doing your best when you don't always feel your best. Bravery is tuning out the universe and trusting your inner voice. Bravery is being yourself. Bravery is speaking out on anything that challenges decency and humanity. It's putting your-self out there for a bigger purpose and picture despite judgment or repercussions. Bravery is pursuing things that are deeply meaningful to you. Some days it feels like things are going to work out and other days not so much, but then you remember why you started, and you keep on anyway. That is bravery! Anything that takes you beyond your comfort zone has a positive effect on your self-esteem. You will realize you're stronger than you think and begin to challenge yourself to climb to new heights. Bravery happens when we decide to show up in our lives.

" *Life* is like a tree shedding its leaves."

UNBECOMING TO BECOME

One day I looked in the mirror and the woman I had seen did not pair up to the woman I had hoped her to be – who I had dreamed her to be. Her morals were all wrong, standards low, and boundaries nonexistent. My father's words kept replaying in my head, "Bry, you're going to be a game changer in this world one day. I pray on it every night", but my behaviors didn't translate into my becoming much. Maybe the journey isn't so much about becoming something or someone, but about unbecoming everything that isn't you so you can be who you are meant to be. Unbecoming, to unravel, breakdown, untangle, and strip away all that no longer serves you or your purpose. One of the easiest ways we fall short of our blessings is by allowing the world to define us before we even get a chance to. It's by committing to the definition of "women speak and behave like this" before we even really know who we are. Creating oneself endlessly and continuously stripping away what you thought you ought to be means changing. Change is uncomfortable. It provokes fear of giving up things, but what we ought to be focused on is all that we have to gain and not what we have to give up I don't know your circumstances. I know very little about you, but one thing I do know is that there is a plan. I know that you and I both were brought here for a reason. I know that our Creator designated each of us with divine purpose, and as we live out our purpose we will go through some good times and some trials - it's all a part of the plan. Our awareness will lead us to know that there are some things we must first un-become.

5
Wildflowers

"Eye *appeasing*, soul pleasing, but also
of overwhelming complexity. *Growing*
in all the places that people never
thought you would."

"Maybe the only way to *heal* is by *forgiving* yourself."

FORGIVE YOURSELF

*O*n this day I am freeing the hostage of my past. I choose to no longer relive and review my mistakes. I am no longer thinking about what I could have done or what the current me would have done. I am thinking about what I will do. I have to remind myself that forgiveness is a good thing. I want to be free from the bitterness and upset I carry. I don't want to be held back from all of the great things my future has to offer me because I have not allowed myself to come to face with the person I was in my past. I know that for a lot of us we spend most of our time working on forgiving others, without ever acknowledging that we need to forgive ourselves. I want this to be a reflective exercise for all of us. If possible, get yourself in front of a mirror so that you can be eye to eye with yourself. I would say something to myself like this, self, I forgive you for the absence of self love. You didn't really know how important you were and nobody really ever told you, but I'm here to show you. I forgive you for the mental and physical self harm you put yourself through. Your new found realization of worthiness will never let you result in such thoughts or actions ever again. The scars on your sleeves and your heart are no longer reflective to the person you are today. It is merely a display that signifies you have overcome. I'm sorry I repeatedly let you go back to the people who've emotionally scorned you. Continue to surround yourself in the company of love, genuinity, and reciprocation. I forgive you. I accept you. Today I move on.

"Life becomes *easier* when you learn to accept the *apology* you'll never get."

IN A HURRY

Be not weary of those who have mishandled us. I was listening to a prophet who told us that we've been mishandled by people who were in a hurry. We don't know exactly where they were trying to run to, or run away from, but they were in a hurry. Nonetheless, we have to forgive them for whatever they did at whatever magnitude. We have to allow ourselves to enter into remission. We may not ever physically hear the words "I am sorry", but we will have to make peace either way. I used to have this pattern of holding on to people who either didn't or couldn't be held. These people were meant to be loved at a distance. I was holding these burdens and these people in my heart for something they did not know they were doing to me. This was so heavy on my spirit and physical being. Instead of allowing that hurt to control me, I do my best to reason with their decisions. I am by no means justifying that if we are in a hurry, it is okay to hurt people along the way, but we should refuse to hold on to that hurt. We empty that hurt and fill the void with other matter that contributes to our well being, such as smiles, and positivity. When we only choose to know light, darkness will no longer affect us. We will be less affected by people who are or aren't in a hurry. Sometimes we have to forgive others for they just do not know.

"It is both a *blessing* and a curse to feel everything so very *deeply*."

I FEEL THINGS

*I*t isn't unusual to feel things and be strongly bonded to the people and things around you. However, society has done a great job of making our ability to clasp emotion a rarity. We pride ourselves on being disconnected or as most call it "numb". Feeling things so deeply is a character attribute that this world needs.. I have feelings; I am sometimes overly sensitive, and I am very content in my emotions. I take full responsibility in how I feel. I don't want to fight it; it's all a part of understanding how I work and who I am. Because of my peculiar sensitivities to my environment, it is habitual for me to share pieces of myself. I want to share my thoughts. I want to give out keys to open up my ""chest" of vulnerability because I understand it is okay for people to see me for me. I feel things, and I'm sure you do too. No matter how hard the people around us try to neglect and" dull" down their emotions, you don't have to do the same. We gain a sense of emotional intellect and maturity when we as people are able to dialogue about the things we feel. Sometimes that is the only missing piece of the puzzle – communication. Those who are dead do not feel so while alive and breathing, do appreciate what you can feel.

"The *connections* between and among women are the most *feared*, the most problematic and the most potentially *transforming* force on the planet."

EMPOWER OUR WOMEN

*I*f you are a woman reading this right now in your teens or twenty-somethings, you are a part of the generations that are diminishing deeply entrenched laws and misguided generalizations that have held back our women for far too long. For far too long we have been in spaces where women compete more than they collaborate, where we hate more than we elevate, and today I would like to draw that line. Women come from generations of oppression – men dictating our careers, our pay, and defining what we should and should not look like. I have made a full effort to stop competing and comparing myself with other women. Instead of undermining and undercutting one another, we can be acknowledging that we are all very talented and all very powerful. There is plenty of space and opportunity for of usl to win. It may feel natural to have your walls up around other women, but make sure on that wall there is a door. A door for other good women to come in and share their love. Some women I have been at odds with for whatever reason have had more in common with me than the women I talk with on a daily basis. When we drop the petty stuff and actually connect, we are surprised at the newly stewed relations. Next time you are out, be the woman in the room to willingly connect with others and drop your guard. Society does enough of picking us apart and putting us against one another. The future is female and when we women unite, we are strong.

"*Differences* are not intended to separate and isolate. We are different in order to realize our need of one *another*."

DIFFERENCES ASIDE

One of the biggest lessons I have ever learned is to find the humanity in everyone. As a minority, you don't always get that treatment, and it's very rare that members of the majority acknowledge it or consider that to be true. We have to be able to put aside stigmas, stereotypes, judgements, biases, and any other irrational thought about others and just see them for who they are – people! We need each other whether we want to believe it or not. I have reason to believe we were put on this earth to help and heal one another, but that's not happening as much as it should be because we tend to acknowledge our differences rather than embrace the fact that we are all just human. I remember being in kindergarten and being assigned a partnered project. Yes, I can remember that far back. What was to be my counterpart was a white girl with blonde hair and blue eyes. She refused to be my partner. When the teacher asked her why, she replied, "I'm not being her partner, she is dirty colored." This obviously isn't a thought that she developed herself. I'm sure she was influenced to believe that, but either way, my kindergarten self was extremely hurt. I didn't know any better other than to think less of myself and the color of my skin when she said that. She didn't see me for me because she saw the color of me, and as a result, she wanted nothing to do with me. We miss out on some great people in our lives by projecting irrational thoughts on them for whatever reason – status, color, possessions, etc. Really give people a chance before you rule them out.

"*Advocacy* is about the stance you take in the public eye. What are you willing to say? What are you *willing* to do?"

TAKE A STAND

As I am I'm writing this, America is under authoritative ruling of someone whose name alone creates division and provokes feelings of anger. His dictation emboldens people to be blatantly hateful and act violently. America is currently everything, but great. I acknowledge that as a nation we have made great strides towards equality, but if you take away our progressiveness we have nothing. Nazi's and white supremacists have been passed off as "very fine people" protected by the 1st amendment, while peaceful protesters have been targeted as "sons of bitches" and deemed unemployable. It is no secret that I am a black woman. I stand for my brothers and sisters, but I also stand for what is right. I stand for women. I stand for human beings. I have faith that as human beings, there will come a day when we can stand together in an indivisible nation, but it is up to us to take a stand. Some reading this are probably thinking "well, this really has nothing to do with me", but it does. If you are on a plane sitting 1st class and a fire breaks out in coach, be prepared to jump because you, my friend, are bound to feel the fire! If we are to be neutral in times of injustice, we have chosen the side of the oppressor. You are our only hope in making a difference in this world. Valencia D. Clay once stated, "Don't throw your fist up in pictures if you're not throwing your fist down in board meetings to open new doors for us. Use your power." It doesn't matter if your neighbor is brown, black, white, pink, orange, or yellow. What good is it if we claim to have faith that humanity can be restored, but no deeds? Take a stand!

"No *beauty* shines brighter than a good *heart.*"

I AM NOT MY POSSESSIONS

I admit I had gotten stuck in the habit of letting my clothes, shoes, cars, and other possessions speak for me. It truly is an ugly and draining life to live. It's exhausting to feel like you always have to keep up in order to be relevant. In addition to painting this daily picture of how great my life was, I wanted to have everything to show for it. The physical things we have in our life wear - they wear out. Our character is what will speak for us forever. Instead of wanting people to see my possessions, I wanted them to see my soul. I knew my soul would have a profound impact on the world far more than things I owned did and even beyond the way I looked. It's not always about looking the part, keeping up with trends, or constantly buying things to show for it. It's about what is beneath the surface that really matters. Society and media will not show you that, but it's true. We see all of these successful people on TV with expensive this and expensive that, but they're not always good people. The casket has room for one – one body. When it is our day to depart this life, will we be known for our good spirits and souls, or just the woman who had uber shoes and handbags? When we leave this earth, let us not be remembered for our possessions, but more for the way that we made others feel.

"Don't let your *fear* of what could happen make *nothing* happen."

FAUX FEAR

*O*verthinking is a critical component of the substance of fear.. A large part of overthinking has always stemmed from my anxiety. Most of the things I have feared in my life have not happened, and I am thankful. If some of them did happen, they weren't nearly as bad as I imagined and that may be because I'm a little dramatic.. For a lot of us, fear is like a leech that constantly sucks the life out of us and confines us within worry and doubt. It's the "what if's" that seem to cloud our sun. Remember when we were younger, we were afraid of the dark. I can't recall a single person I've met who wasn't. It wasn't so much the dark that frightened us, but the endless possibilities our mind had made up of what could lie in the darkness. We unknowingly live our lives inside the boundaries that our fears establish. We operate out of the fearfulness of failure, rejection, criticism, and judgment. Addressing and overcoming your fears or what you think you fear has a lot to do with being consciously aware of your fears. We have to be willing to take the necessary steps in letting go in order to be set free. That may mean putting a greater emphasis on not only exercising our bodies, but exercising our minds. Prayer, meditation, and solitude have all helped me increase my levels of awareness. It has also given me the power to have confidence in my capabilities in order to overcome my fears. What are you willing to do and what measures will you take to be released from the strains of your fears?

"When someone *shows* you who they are, *believe* them."

THE COLORS ARE AS THEY APPEAR

*T*here is a very popular quote you might have heard from the late Maya Angelou, and it goes "the first time someone shows you who they are, believe them." I like to think of this theory as a revelation of true colors. It is an important lesson in life, but most of you may agree that we do not always apply it to everyone we encounter. I think about the many times this specific quote has applied to the people I've trusted. I think about why I allowed so many opportunities for others to cross me. With age, you tend to tolerate a lot less. I now pay more attention to energy and intentions. It's evident that we can apply this lesson to all sorts of relations, but for me, it's most prevalent in the light of friendships. When I look back, I can see the revelation of true colors from individuals I sought out be my "friend". I had a friend who was like a walking newspaper. She knew everyone's business, and she wasn't discrete about any of it no matter who you were. I thought it genuinely had to be an accident when she repeated some of the things I shared with her, but then her excessive talking became habitual. Then I started telling her a lot less, and finally I stopped talking to her. I don't think that it means she is necessarily a bad person, but I should have noticed that I couldn't trust her much earlier and known that the problem was serious. What drew me to make that mistake is I wanted her to be that friend I could go to in confidence, and I felt in my heart that she had the potential to be that person. I should have believed her the first time she showed me exactly who she was. Have you ever dealt with anything similar where you've dismissed a person's wrongdoings because of her potential? More often than not, we just have to see the colors as they appear and keep it moving.

"*Envy* comes from people's ignorance of, or lack of belief in *themselves.*"

SNAKES IN THE GRASS

*I*f you thought high school was catty and full of unnecessary drama, it's possible that some of those same people will carry those tendencies into college or their careers. When I got to college, I was very shy and reserved. I didn't really have many problems because I spent most of my time to myself, went to school, went to practice, and I guess no one really saw that as threatening. I found a mentor who pushed me to get involved and engaged with my community. I met some beautiful people along the way. I also met some people who weren't really a fan of my stepping out of my shell. Till this day, I can't really put my thumb on the exact reason why it bothers some people to see you win. That's the reality of things. On your journey you will have genuine support and sadly you will have others who are praying on your downfall. Support comes in many variations including "those who want to see you do great, but not better than them." Be weary of the snakes in the grass and move accordingly. People bothered by your success has more to do with them than it does with you. No matter how much or how little you feel like you're being supported or falsely supported, continue to make your stamp on the universe because what matters the most is your growth and the legacy you leave behind.

"Your *excuses* are just the lies you tell yourself to feel *better*."

EXCUSES ARE TOOLS OF INCOMPETENCE

*E*xcuses in my heart pain more than lies. They change nothing, but make everyone telling these lies feel better. It's almost like a comfort cushion when we feel like we may fail at something. When we make excuses, we usually make more excuses than we make progress. I used to be overweight and came up with every reason why I would stay overweight and out of shape. Maybe it's genetics, a number of people in my family are fairly large. It's my dad's fault. He takes me to McDonalds all the time, how could I possibly say no to that? I just don't have enough time. What are those excuses?. You see how I have found a way to blame everyone and everything, but myself? Nowhere in this story did I take responsibility or even acknowledge the fact that something needed to change. I just kept on with my excuses. We have to stop making excuses. Instead, we must make things happen and leave our print on the world. Eventually, I got myself together and made my health a priority. All because I realized excuses change nothing. Change and the will to do anything start from within.

You will figure out that what you want badly enough, you will do just about anything to get it or get there. All of a sudden the excuses are less and the work ethic is up! Excuses inhibit us from winning.

"The man who *throws* two stones
misses the *target*."

MULTITASKING IS A SCAM

*O*ne of the laws of life is that whatever we give our energy to, something else gets a little less of our energy. We have to break our complex list of goals into small attainable tasks. Start by doing one thing at a time. This will allow us time to put our soul into it with the exclusion of all other things. Sometimes it's good to step back and just focus on one task at a time. We can do that to ensure we're engaged, giving our best selves, and putting forth optimum effort. What are you currently working on? If it's more than one item, ask what matters most to you? Water it, tend to it , shed your light solely on that one thing and watch it blossom. Once it blossoms, we can tend to our other flowers. Giving 50 50 is only giving half of yourself to each task. Putting your all and maximum effort into something require all of your attention but often ends with superb results. Multitasking is one of the biggest fibs we've ever told ourselves. Being busy doesn't always mean we are being productive. Use a Step by step method and do one thing at a time and know that something is always better than nothing.

"If you aim at *nothing*, you'll hit it *every* time."

CAN YOU REMEMBER?

*T*ake some time to think about where you've been investing your thoughts, time, and energy. Can you remember the commitments you made to yourself? How are you tracking? I was in church today, and our reverend was speaking to us about resolutions. She said "every January all of you make a New Year's resolution. Most of you, today, probably don't even remember your resolution." Things come up or things go wrong, and we fall by the wayside and completely forget about those resolutions we made at the beginning of the year. We still have time. We still have time to recommit. If you're like me and by now have forgotten all about those commitments you made, we still have time to make new ones. Write them down this time! People who write down their clear goals tend to accomplish far more in a short period of time than people without them could ever imagine. The wonderful thing about life is that in every breathing moment, we can make many commitments, goals, or to-do lists. The New Year is not the only day we sit down and goal plan. Even if you can't remember your initial promises you made to yourself, remember this… Every day you open your eyes and are granted breath is a day you can recommit, set goals, and set out to do all you desire.

"*Before* you can break out, you must acknowledge that you are locked up, and then *reason* with how you got there."

ADDICTION

*I*t's not your fault. I just have to start off by telling you it's not your fault. If you are or have ever dealt with a relative, parent, friend, or significant other dealing with addiction, it is not your fault. Addiction is much bigger than you and I. These drugs nowadays are advanced and addictive. Addiction supersedes love, care, and all other relationship components. Anyone who is addicted will constantly fulfill that need. Valencia D. Clay once said, "If you know the feeling of being neglected by someone who chose to get high over spending time with you, you know how hard it is to love yourself." It's not that the person dealing with dependency loves us any less; it's that the addiction is much more powerful than anything else. People constantly use drugs to dismiss their deeply distressing experiences without realizing the effect it has on their daughters, mother, sisters, etc. Drugs take you to a hell that'll temporarily feel like heaven. Addiction does not always kill the addict, but the people who care. Nobody ever took the time to sit me down and explain addiction and how it overpowers everything in your life. I've spent years in regret thinking to myself "what could I have done to prevent this?" I've spent years trying to forgive. I've spent years trying to heal from the abandonment, but the most important thing I have come to understand is that it is not my fault. You can't help a person who doesn't want to be helped, and you can't help people who are making no effort to help themselves. You don't deserve to be in the crossfire of things until they figure it out.

"Say *yes* to others, as long as you are not saying no to *yourself*."

IT'S OKAY TO
SAY NO

*T*here are times I feel this gigantic pressure to do all sorts of things I would rather not do. I'm thinking about all the things I have to do, would like to do, and the things others would like me to do on top of everything else.There's so much guilt followed by saying "no". We are hesitant to say "no" because of the possible backlash we'll receive. We think people will judge us. There's a possibility we might upset the person we are telling no. Nobody likes the person who continues to tell them no, right? I understand. Here's my truth... I was in the season of telling people yes all of the time. The thought of saying no to the people I cared about haunted me, but I often regretted saying "yes". Saying "yes" all the time gets exhausting, and it's unrealistic. It takes a hit on our mental, physical, and spiritual health. Saying "yes" too much will take a toll on our priorities as well. Our happiness streams from the choices we make on a day to day basis. If you're not sure, don't have the time, it doesn't interest you, or are juggling a million and one things on your plate, it's okay to say no. Don't stress yourself out by stretching yourself. Good friends and colleagues will understand. It's okay to say no because that means we have a better understanding of our limits.

"You know the *value* of every article of merchandise you own, but without the knowledge of the *value of your soul* - it's all nonsense."

VALUE

A well known speaker started off his seminar holding up a crisp perfectly pressed twenty dollar bill and asked his class, "who wants it?" Everyone shot up their hands yelling, "Me! I want it! Give it to me!" with so much excitement. He then crumpled the twenty dollar bill up in his hand and asked the class, "well, who wants it now?" Every hand was raised again with the same level of excitement. The man threw the twenty dollar bill on the ground where he proceeded to stomp on it and wipe his feet back and forth on the bill. The class was looking at him in concern unsure of what he could possibly be doing. When he posed the question again, everyone was slow to raise a hand; nonetheless, everyone's hand was raised. We have all learned a very valuable lesson today. No matter what the speaker did to the money, we still wanted it because although the bill had been rumpled and stepped on, it did not decrease in value. Through our adversities, there may be times when we feel that we are worthless. No matter what has or will occur, we will never lose our value.

"It's okay to be *scared*, but you have to get out there, open up, love, make mistakes, learn, and start *all over* again."

TEENAGE FEVER

I remember dating in my teens. I remember the very first time I fell in love. Teenage love is complicated yet very intriguing. I can describe all other types of love the same way, but those descriptions are very true for teenage love. Teenage love is all about discovery. It's when most of us are just getting our feet wet with connection, partnership, and how to get a handle on all of these newly evoked emotions. The first time I was ever allowed to date and gave love a try, I thought it was everything that I had been missing in life. When I felt like I found my equal, I felt like I had the world in my hands and that it was something/someone I never wanted to let go. We were so young, but nobody could tell us that it wasn't love. We started growing out of one another. Curiosity seeped into our relationship, and there was just so much about life that we had yet to figure out on our own. Needless to say more, we broke up. One thing I know about teenage love gone wrong is that it sucks. When I look back on how distraught I was, I literally laugh, but I was torn. Your first boyfriend or girlfriend may or may not be your "forever" and that is okay. The same thing I told my little cousin was the same thing I wish my elders would've told me and kept reminding me. "When you get to college, it will be a whole new ball game", I used to tell her. I was right.

Teenage years are the years of discovery in almost everything. If things don't workout, there is no need to lose ourselves in what feels like defeat. There will be more opportunities, maybe even better opportunities, and definitely more life.

"It is not until you *know* better that you can do *better*."

YOUR TWENTY-SOMETHINGS

I mentioned earlier that our teen years are more of our discovery years. We are trying to find out who we are and discover our niche in this world. Our twenty-somethings are the years to go get it. They are the years of drive and pursuing a life that is not only sustainable, but a life that is better than the one yesterday. It's not a time for continuous compromise, but it is a time to put you first. We are going upward, forward, and in these moments people are either with us or in the way. Our twenty-somethings aren't always necessarily our best years. Sometimes they're painful and staggering. We are the seeds doing our best with what we have while trying to sprout out from the ground. It's not the time to be so fixated on finding a spouse. It's not the era of comparison. There's a lot of pressure to be fully bloomed in your twenty-somethings, but that just isn't right. When we migrate from our teens to our twenties, the transition is all about the seed planting. We are still growing. There's such a misconception in "fully bloomed" because most living organisms will grow forever. The foundation we build in our twenties will define us forever. So it's not necessarily about having it all together by the time you're twenty-something, but it's about doing what it takes in your twenty-somethings to secure the life you've been dreaming of.

"The *body* is your first and last
garment; it is what you *enter* life in and
what you *depart* life with."

MY TEMPLE

Sharing your body with yourself is a journey of its own. As we grow, we spend a decent amount of time over analyzing every inch – the parts we love and the others we don't. We are literally like unplucked and untouched flowers at one point, and once squeezed in hand, there is an inability to return to their initial state. That's how precious and intimate sex is. So when I say "my temple", I mean nothing more and nothing less. We have to start treating our bodies as sacred; home of our breath, mind, and soul. By no means am I telling you what to do with your body, but I would like you to know it's not for everybody. Once touched, we can't be untouched, and that is something I had to learn the hard way. Now that I know who I am and have a complete understanding of my worth, I would rather explore my temple with someone I completely trust. This someone must equally respect me and holds me in high regards. I need someone who attends to me, water me, and will not pluck me from my roots unless I say so. To whom are we giving these experiences? I've shared pieces of me with others who've made me wish I shared nothing at all and brought hesitancy to the idea of sharing with anyone else. Our bodies are our temples for the soul. So be wary of soul ties to people who don't wish to garden you.

"Ride the *waves*, move with the sea,
let the sounds of the water set your
soul *free*."

FISH IN THE SEA

*L*ove is an emotional roller coaster. It is a ride I personally need breaks from, but the same ride I always come back to for another ride. The interesting thing about amusement parks is that we hear these dreaded stories about roller coaster accidents and incidents all the time, and we are cautioned about getting on that specific roller coaster, but it doesn't necessarily stop us from exploring others. Love is the same way. Teenage love gone wrong feels like the ride of no return. All loves after that are pretty much trial and error. That's the thing we do not communicate enough with one another. The truth of the matter is if you loved once, you can love again. There are plenty of fish in the sea, and although we end up with a few bad catches that force us to throw them back, we will have occasion to catch a few that we won't let go. We can't let the breakdown of the rides or the few bad catches deter us away from the water of the world – love. To love and be loved is what keeps Mother Earth spinning. Don't let any particular fish bring you away from that because there are plenty of fish in the sea –eight billion to be exact.

"Music is the *therapy* our hearts call out for. It connects people in ways that *no other* medium can."

MUSIC MAKES MEMORIES

When I hear a song, I can always date what year that came out because of whatever I was going through at the time. Sometimes these melodies paint some of the most blissful illustrations in my mind. These are the songs that we love. They become wrapped in a neural quilt uniquely patched with people, specific locations, and weather adjustments throughout our life. There is a science behind this, but it is beautiful that we all can experience. When I hear songs from the early 2000's, I feel free. I am an evolving child. I have my first boyfriend. I have my first heartbreak. I am unapologetically dancing without fear of judgment or the pains of how ridiculous I might look. Early 2000's music brings me back to serenity and freedom. Life was good. When you hear older tunes, what memories surface on your brain? Are they good times? Are they bad times? There's a part in our brain designated to motions, emotions, and creativity. We live through music – having different theme songs that totally align with whatever we were growing through then and now. Music has the capability of lifting our spirits. Music is not only something that connects us, but it is a gift that helps us remember. Through some of my traumatic experiences, I simply cannot remember some of the most precious times in my life. The gift of music is what always brings me back. It will always bring us all back.

"The only *mistake* you can make is not asking for *help*."

ASK FOR HELP

Are you comfortable asking for help? When we reach a certain age, we start super-womaning through our days trying to do it all on our own, myself included. There used to be an insecurity that ticked in me when I asked for help. That or I subconsciously self righteously think that I can do it all on my own. The truth is, sometimes I need help. You probably do too! The news is, it's okay to ask for help! When we ask for help, it may feel like we are losing a little control of the situation or task. That's not the case. I have found out that including others in my projects not only levitates some of my stress, but it gives me another perspective. When I include others or ask for help, they usually tell me if I am producing quality work. If I am not, we can brainstorm together to make sure not only does it get done, but that I am putting forth my best work. I've only been on this earth for about twenty something years. When I have a question, I'm going to someone with years of expertise. I let go of my ego. I realize I don't know everything. If there is ever a time I get an opportunity to learn from someone who's been doing what I am doing now, I will listen. I know now that asking for help doesn't diminish my capabilities. It simply empowers me.

"One small *crack* does not mean you are broken; it means that you were put to the *test*, and you didn't fall apart. You didn't *fail*."

BENT NOT BROKEN

Adversity has a way of defining us. It tells us a lot about who we are and who we are to become. There are days when we are knocked down, walked over, or as I would like to call it "bent". One thing we mustn't allow ourselves to be is broken. When our backs are against the wall, will we fold, will we fall, or will we prevail? I have cried out of fear of being broken, but I laugh now knowing that the sadness I had felt was only temporary. I wasn't broken at all. Pain hurts like a cut from a knife continuously carving those same wounds, but once the knife is removed those wounds have an opportunity to heal. It's just a matter of removing the knife. How can we remove the knife? We can't pin it down to just one answer, but there is always a way to remove the knife and there will always be a chance for us to repair and heal. Sometimes we have to get knocked down to our lowest in order to stand back up taller than we ever were. Joy and love are the aloe coming to kiss and seal your wounds, and from that day you will understand you were never broken, just bent.

"The greatest *contribution* you can make to women's rights, is to be the absolute *best* you that you can be."

I OWE YOU

When I think about women like Sirimavo Bandaranaike, Mae Carol Jemison, Wilma Mankiller, Junko Tabei, and Susan B. Anthony, I think of phenomenal women who have paved a way for women today. All of these women have given us rights or set some type of standard that allows us to be who we are today. We aren't always mindful of the strenuous work it took to open this gateway of women's rights. Sometimes I find myself taking it for granted. Education, job opportunities, voting, and owning property were all things that at one time women thought were unattainable. I remember hearing stories from my grandmother on how the women listened to their men and didn't have much of an opinion or life outside of that. Each generation of women has a responsibility to the next one. We owe it to the women before us to make an impact on generations to come. What do you want to pass on? Next time you read, vote, go to work, and wear a pair of slacks, pause for a moment and put a "thank you" into the universe for the women who came before us and created great change in order for us to live the lives we live today. We owe it to them to not only take full advantage of what we are afforded, but we must continue to keep carving at gender equality.

" *Life* is a matter of choices, and every choice you make has it's way of making *you*."

THE CHOICE IS YOURS

How many decisions do you make throughout an entire day? A ton! Sometimes, We probably make decisions without even knowing it. Some choices are bigger than others; some choices affect us directly, and other choices affect us indirectly. No matter how small or grand the choice, it matters. Having choices is both a blessing and a curse. If we make enough good choices, we can surely expect great results. If, over time, we make enough bad choices, we can expect to pay the price. We often miss out on all of the power that lies within having the ability to choose. We often think of it as powerfulness in terms of rewards, but we don't consider the power within us to decide – to choose anything, good, or bad. Nothing great happens overnight. I'm sure nothing bad does either. My pastor told me "an overweight person doesn't become obese from one overly proportioned meal. They become obese by a number of great meals overtime." You all might be thinking why in the heck is your pastor talking to you about weight? What he was trying to get to is that it's not one choice today that will affect our future. It is the choices we consistently make over time that determine our destiny. Continue to make good choices. When it comes to the smallest decision or grandest decision, even when nobody is watching, make good choices. Success doesn't come from what's done occasionally. It comes from what is done constantly.

"It takes time to *succeed* because success is merely the natural reward for taking the *time* and putting in the time."

OPRAH WASN'T BUILT IN A DAY

I often tend to use this slogan as a self reminder to emphasize that significant matters take time. We can't expect important things to come about in a short period of time. I had to master my hyper development phases. If it were not a lack of funds getting in the way of making my dreams a reality, it was surely something else. Oprah wasn't built in a day. If you know anything about Oprah's life, you know that she has endured a lot, but she has risen over the odds. Ideally, you have most likely heard the phrase, "Rome wasn't built in a day." I am telling you the same thing but with a twist on it. Although both statements are true, all great things and people take time to develop. While keeping perspective on your dream, remember there's more to it. "Rome wasn't built in a day, but they were laying bricks every hour" – as was Oprah. Sometimes we fantasize about the empire without putting into perspective the laborious work it takes to build the empire. Lay bricks – every day, every month, every year. That's how you build your inner Oprah. That's how you build your empire. Take your time, appreciate the journey, and really take it in – all great things take time.

"If one *person* that looks like you made it, then you can too. If one person from your town made it, you *made it too.*"

SUCCESS IN THE CITY

*T*here are two types of people in this world. Those who become better because of the success stories around them and then there are those who become bitter. In my eyes, my mother was a city success in her prime. She had an in-home daycare, a security company, did event coordinating, booking, and management for local talent. Before she lost control, my image of success and being a girl boss was my mother. After that, and even now, I look for every possible connection between myself and other successful women. With all of my fellow small town folks aspiring to move away because of the lack of opportunities, it was and still is significant when I see people within my city win. I get great surges of confidence when I hear about all of the success stories and people from my home state. I know several women from back home that are involved and beyond successful in so many different avenues. It makes me light up! We have women who are philanthropist, teachers, lawyers, doctors, athletes, artists, boutique owners, fashion designers, musicians, fitness enthusiasts, and so much more. Not only does it make me light up to see them work, but it motivates me to be better and more purposeful. I receive affirmation that lets me know that flowers are able to bloom wherever they're planted. It also ratifies that there is room for all of us. There is a seat at the table for all of us. Sharing success stories is one of the most important things we can do to motivate and inspire each other. Success is so incredibly important to all of us, but representation resonates on a totally different level. Don't find yourself looking at other people's work and wondering "why not me" because it easily can be you. Allow your city success stories to fuel you and permit you to take away a much deeper commitment to support one another.

6
Bloom

"Sometimes you have to *let go* of
all that you thought you were to fully
bloom into the *woman* you are meant
to be, and when you get there, own it.
Own your light and *all that you are.*"

"You are able to tell a *tree* by the fruit it bares and man by his deeds. He who plants *kindness* grows in love."

RANDOM ACTS OF KINDNESS

Random acts of kindness seem to have somewhat gotten away from us.. The lack of generally comes from the idea that the person receiving might not appreciate your kind gestures. Their apprehensive behavior reflects a person who distrusts and sadly this speaks to the world's current social standing. More people need to be kind to one another. Being kind is such a rarity that some may not digest it as genuine and instead negate it with skepticism. The cure for this is more random acts of kindness done by all of us, and it starts with me and you. We have to be willing to give to those fortunate, those not so fortunate, those that love us, and those that don't love us – yes, those that don't love us. Give two times more to those you do not want to give to. Random acts of kindness will liberate you from selfishness, isolation, and self-absorption. Giving without the intent of receiving is the true gem, and you never know how important your giving may be to the person you are giving to. I once spent my work day in a Panera where an elderly man had walked in off the street. From his appearance of carrying multiple bags, I could assume he had been on the street for a while. He filled up his coffee mug and took a bunch of napkins back to his seat. I went over to him and handed him some paper. His face lit up as if I just handed him gold. He later came back and handed me back a paper that read "multumesc" which means thank you in Romanian. What was so simple for me meant the greatest of gestures to him. Something so simple as paper. We don't know the different demons other people are dealing with, but we have the power to bring joy and potentially even change their life with random acts of kindness. Make an effort to indulge in random acts of kindness. That extension of love, selflessness, and compassion that you put out will find its way back to you.

"I want to *inspire* people. I want
someone to look at me and say
"because of you, I did not *give up*"

BE AN INSPIRATION TO OTHERS

*I*t doesn't take much to find people who inspire us, but the difficulty comes in being an example and inspiration to others. Some of us have this narrative in mind that we have to be someone who is constantly successful, organized, and able to manage life's task – all while looking like we have it all together and figured out, but that is not true. People out there are looking for someone who is genuine and authentic. They are looking for people to bare their truth. There was a time in my life when I did what I could with the minimal that I had. I wasn't making the best decisions or hiding the fact that I was struggling, but I was surviving to the best of my ability. There were a lot of people who didn't expect anything great to become of me, and very few people offered assistance. There were others going through like situations – doing what they could with the very minimal they had, and I saw them watching me. Ten years later, I made it out of the" rut." One of the greatest rewards was someone telling me "because of you, I didn't give up" or "because of you, I am now trying something different." The magnitude of your impact is most often determined by your ability to get things done or make it through in your most troubling times. You never know who is watching, but the possibility of people aspiring to do what you do and watching you do it is likely. When things get hard, know that there are others out there who are going through it too. The little eyes are watching, and they're depending on your victory to lift them up.

"How you make them *feel* will always hold more weight than words you *said*."

THE GOLDEN RULE

For many of us, in our early childhood development, we were lectured with "the golden rule". If you weren't constantly reminded of it by your educators, it was sure to be displayed in one of the classrooms we sat in. What is the golden rule? The golden rule is to treat people the way we would like to be treated, but I don't think it is in great enough detail. How we treat people, especially the most vulnerable, is a revelation of our true identity. It says more about who you are than what you are telling people about yourself. Our truest colors seem to show when we are in the presence of others who are not exactly like us. They can be of a different class, ethnicity, sexual orientation, sex, and the list goes on. What I really want to bring to the surface is how we treat those who may be different from us and are in need. Are we quick to do what we can for others despite our differences? Do the social stereotypes make us a little apprehensive to lend a helping hand? Be honest with yourself .I will admit that sometimes I've subconsciously been a little hesitant to extend myself. I realize that doing nothing for a person in need is just as bad as doing something to them. So not only should we treat people the way in which we would like to be treated, but we should put all biases aside and be sure to help those in need. If there is something you can do about it, do it!

"Be of those *few* who walk because
most people only *talk*."

EVIDENCE

Plenty of people will tell us what they do without our actually seeing it. It's fair to say that sometimes we all need a little more than to hear about good works, but we need to be able to see it – evidence. I am not a person that generally talk a lot about what I do because I would rather the people I am trying to reach, see it. I want them to feel it and so should you. We have to put forth the evidence that we are who we claim to be. We not only talk the talk, but we also walk the walk. The only thing undoubtedly proving that is our actions, our works, and our impact we have on other people or the things around us. Talk is cheap. I was in church one day and my pastor was delivering a sermon. He paused for a minute and stated "we can tell a tree by the fruit it bares. There are plenty of people who claim they are rooted in good faith, intention, and spirits. Hypothetically speaking, some will even claim to be an apple tree, but sooner than later the proof will or will not be on the limbs of that tree." Not only should we be weary of those who do not provide us enough evidence, but we need to make sure we are not only saying what we do, but doing what we say.

" *Live* the way you want to be
remembered."

LEAVING A LEGACY

*T*he discussion of leaving a legacy behind has come up with my partner and I. We are both in our early twenties so we thought about this concept when approaching our college graduation. His vision solely focused on his basketball career while mine focused on the people I had encountered. Our visions of leaving a legacy behind at our alma mater would have everything to do with how we wanted to be remembered and what we had contributed to our institution. I had hoped that during my years at Shaw University, I had impacted as many people as I possibly could. I believe I did. My selflessness and service became my legacy. Although I was buried in being a student athlete and other extra curricular activities, I always made it a priority to help whoever wanted to be helped. I do not think I would have been as successful during my collegiate career without investing in others. What will your legacy be? What will people remember about you ? We figure out our legacies by reflecting and defining what is important to us. For me, it was important for me to not only set myself up for success, but assure the path for others. When we are gone, people will have a story to tell about us and the way in which we would like that story to be told depends on what we do today. It's never too late to start making a difference and setting the foot stones for your legacy. What legacy will you be leaving?

"Don't *underestimate* me. I know more than I say, think more than I speak, and notice more than you *realize*."

LET THEM SLEEP

*T*he me I am today is not who I was several years ago. If you were to go and ask a majority of the people who knew me in my past life, I bet some of them would say they had no expectations of my being as achieved as I am today. There will be individuals who don't see your full potential. There will be people who will laugh at you and "dull down" your dreams. These are the people that I like to say are "sleeping" on you. The kicker is, let them sleep. Yes, let them sleep! Someone once stated that there will be people that you will experience throughout your lifetime that will be unsure and have doubts about you and will be sleeping on you. Let them sleep. Let those people sleep before they wake up and be in your way. As your success starts to reveal itself, those people will surprisingly wake up and do just that – be in your way. They will be ready to be involved and proud to say they knew or know you. Some will even be irritated by your success. There is no need to address those who were once naysayers, just keep winning. The world has a humorous way of revealing authentic support. In your pursuits, there will be enough genuine support to overflow the fake clapping, and you won't be phased by the sleepers.. Let them sleep on you!

"Fun doesn't *stop* just because you're a little *older* now."

GIRLS JUST WANT TO HAVE FUN

How many days out of the week are you actually having fun? I mean real fun, smiling ear to ear, and filling your space with laughter. How many days are you really guaranteed? We never exactly know. Let us get off of whatever edge we are on and make a promise today to enjoy life. At least try to. We don't have to make everything so serious. If things aren't fun in your life right now, create it. Cast out what everyone else will say about your journey to new joys and just do it. Growing up I was so fearful of not being successful and stable that I missed out on my childhood. When I reconnect with old friends, there are so many joyful memories shared that I just wasn't a part of because I took life way too serious. It wasn't necessarily a bad thing, but it is healthy to be engaged in matter from time to time that contribute to your laughter and your happiness. My boyfriend has to check me from time to time to ensure I am making time for my joy. I appreciate that about him. He makes an effort to say something when he sees I am physically burying myself in all of my work. I'm glad I made it a point to include fun ventures into my life. Hang out with the people that will make you want to put your phone down, forget about work, and the rest of the worries of your world. We only get one life to enjoy. I don't want to reach my peak ages and wish that I would've enjoyed myself more in my youth because at that moment I will realize that is not time I can get back, and life didn't always have to be so serious.

"So fill your *heart* with what's important and be done with the *rest*."

LESSONS IN LIFE

I love social media in the retrospect that it's like our own little universe to communicate and share almost anything we want. I was on twitter recently and ran into a mason jar exercise a teacher was doing with his students. The teacher would place an empty jar on his desk. It was then filled with ping pong balls. The teacher asked his students "is the jar full yet?" The students all agreed that it was. From the visual, you could see that despite the ping pong balls being piled to the top of the jar, there was still space in the jar. He then poured beads into the jar. Those beads filled all of the spaces between the ping pong balls. He asked the students again "is the jar full?" The students were sure this time it had to be full. So the teacher proceeded to pour sand in the jar.The sand filled all the space that was left. When everyone assumed the jar was finally full, the teacher started pouring beer inside the mason jar. The sand quickly soaked all of the beer. He turned to his students and said, "this jar represents your life. The balls are the truly important stuff (love, health, friends, and family). While the beads are the secondary things (your car, job, and your home). Think of the sand as a representation of all the small stuff in your life. If we were to pour the sand first, we wouldn't have any room for the beads and the balls.The same thing happens in our life. So pay attention to the things that are most critical to your happiness." A student later asked what the beer represented, and the teacher explained "no matter how full your life may be, there is always room for a beer with a friend". Hopefully this was a college lecture, but of course you get the point.

"Only *you* can change your life.
No one can do it for *you*."

IT'S UP TO ME

*I*t's so hard to see the bigger picture when your vision is restricted by obstacles. The obstacles and hardships we are currently facing often inhibit us from seeing or thinking ahead. What we sometimes fail to realize is that we possess the power to change our lives. Nobody possesses the power to change our circumstances like we do. The change will always start within, and it will always start with us. Whether it be our health, our income, our relationships – those changes start with us. We have to start creating new habits and moving differently and that all starts with a choice. Decide your fate today. It's never too late. The beauty about life is that as long as we are alive, we still have the ability to determine our experiences and determine our fate. I wasn't always the best and most attentive student and my high school GPA reflected that. Of course that made it very hard for me to get accepted into schools, but thankfully I got another chance. I had already had it made up in my mind that if I were given another chance, I would take full advantage, and really apply myself. I graduated from high school with a 2.7 GPA and little enthusiasm about what my future held. With a change of habits and some social sacrifices, I managed to graduate from college with a 3.1 GPA. Aside from God, I take full credit for that. One day I woke up and made a decision to do better because I wanted a better life. It's up to us!

"The *reward* for conformity is that everyone likes you except *yourself*."

DO NOT CONFORM

I like to think that each of us was brought to this earth in our own unique design and with great detail. Not one of us is the exact same and not one of us serves the exact same purpose. Whatever that purpose is, stick to it! I think a lot of us have a habit of getting caught up in what society wants us to be, how society wants us to look, or even the life that our parents have already mapped out for us the day we came out of the womb. I have one thing to say about that, do not conform! As we progress in our years, I can only pray that the universe continues to grow to be more inclusive and less demanding on placing everyone in a box of should and should nots.. I like to consider conformity as our prison of freedom and the archenemy of growth. Conformity is part of the systematic slavery that still exists because once they are able to conform us, they are able to control us. Be you and live rich in your individuality. The only way to live a full life is by filling it with the things that make us passionate and meet our individual needs. In order to love yourself, you have to be just that – yourself. Corporate America has taught me that there are women in corporate who look just like me, but do everything they can to be less of themselves. Their idea of belonging is to physically replicate the majority, and I just can't get down with that. I refuse to do anything that is unnatural to me or my roots for the sake of fitting in. More importantly, I refuse to conform because I know what I bring to the table. We need women who don't quite fit into the stereotype to confidently climb the corporate ladder as they are, and we also need more women accepting them. With or without your willingness to conform, you are strong. You are worthy and your contribution to whatever environment you're in will speak for itself.

"The will and *desire* to win, the urge to reach your full potential… these are the keys that will *unlock* the door to great achievement and personal *excellence*."

THOSE WHO WORK, WIN

Have you ever been so driven and motivated to do something that you sacrifice it all? Sacrifice your social life, sleep, and sometimes even eating because you are are so concentrated! Sometimes that's what it takes to win. When we look at other women like Beyoncé, we know that she has been working to get to where she is her entire life. Winning doesn't come easy and it usually doesn't happen overnight. If you're expecting the overnight success or miracle to happen, cut it out. Knock it off. It will take a different strength to get to where we want to be in life. When others are asleep, we need to be the ones up and working. Keep in mind that this doesn't mean we necessarily have to work harder, but let's work smarter and really put in the time. Wake up earlier to have more hours in the day to tend to your dream. These are all the things we have to do to win. We have to work. If what you are after is something that you love, then forget trying to compete or outdo yourself. You will be READY to work because that's how much you love it! You will be WILLING to work because that's how much you love it! Nobody will be able to stop you because that fire in your eyes, and in your heart, will fuel you to keep putting in that work until you get the results you want. The price of your dreams is hard work. You are fully equipped and ready to win, but for that to happen you don't only have to prepare to win, but you must expect to win.

"Life is either a *daring* adventure
or *nothing* at all."

RISK

I had an esteemed woman once tell me "the higher the risk, the greater the reward." Then I thought to myself, how many opportunities have I missed out on because I was afraid to take a risk? On top of that, one word stuck out to me like pink at a funeral... "afraid". Fear is what stops us from taking risk and often times has us missing out on great things in life. Of course risk taking inherently has "loser" written all over it, but one day we have to start taking risks and gradually letting go of our fears. As you know, great things never come from comfort zones. So start taking it too far in order to discover how far it is you can actually go. We are able to let go of the worry in the risk when we focus on what it is we gain instead of what we could lose. Would you agree that more times than not, the gain is monumental compared to whatever it is you could lose? See! Years from now you will be more affected by the things you didn't do than the things you've done. It's risky. It's scary. There's a huge chance it won't work out, but guess what? Do it anyway! What doesn't always work out will give us the wisdom to come back and do better. On the other side of fear is everything we've ever wanted in life.

"I got my *own* back."

YOUR #1 FAN

Are you your number one fan? If you are not, what is holding you back? Think about when nobody is around or you're taking your time in isolation. The most important relationship we have in our lifetime is the one we have with ourselves. No matter what life may throw at you, it is you who has to deal with it. It is you that will always be with yourself. Over the years, being my own #1 fan was difficult. There were many days when I would break down. There were many days when I was sad in loneliness, but I knew if I wanted to overcome the pain and accomplish anything I needed to comfort myself. I needed to support myself the way that I support these celebrities that I don't know a thing about. I had to motivate myself. It is a journey, and I'm still on the road learning myself every day. I can say that I've gotten better. At this very moment, I would say that I am my #1 fan. I deserve the same love and courage I give others and you do also. You will find that by becoming your own #1 fan, validation and acceptance are no longer a concern of yours because the only approval you will need is your own. Be gentle, be kind, and be everything to yourself that you want from others. Be your own #1 fan.

"New *friends* bring new
energy to your *soul*."

NO NEW FRIENDS

When you're up, it's always funny to see who starts showing up, who wants to turn up, and who finds a way in your space. For that exact reason, many of us have been very cautious about new friends. I recently read Charlamagne, Tha God's book, "Black Privilege". In the book, he mentions Drake's song, "No New Friends," that sends a hit and miss message to avoid making new friends. No new friends, right? Wrong! A large percent of what I've achieved in my career is due to the new friends I have made along the way. It bothers me when some of my peers are less willing to intermingle and make new connections. That's an absolute way to block potential blessings. I understand that we should not make ourselves easily accessible to just anybody, but some of us are building walls that are blocking great things from entering. If I solely relied on all of the people I considered "day one", do you know how lost I'd be? If you have any friends from "day one" that still exhibit the same mindset that they had when you both were young, let that friend go and hope that friend grows! That's the last place you need to be looking for advice and assistance. Nonetheless, your friends should fuel you. You will find that a friend you meet today could be more loyal and purposeful than a friend you've had for years.

"To me *beauty* is being comfortable in your own skin. It's about *knowing* and *accepting* who you are."

I AM A
MASTERPIECE

We women are like art. The architect and creator give us purpose, and not one of us is the same, but we acquire fine commonalities. We are delightful; we are strong, and we attribute to procreation. Not only are we appeasing to the eye, but we are important. Mankind would be wiped without us. The creator took time on us. Each line, scar, stretch mark, wrinkle and roll surfaced with intent. It's supposed to be there. All of this personality with a physical presence to match is specific. It's exhilarating! These things shape me to be, me. I am a masterpiece. I need not to compete because I am already complete. Like art, I come with perception. There will be eyes that do not understand and that will undervalue. These misconceptions come from those who cannot control us. They will try to control how others view us as well, but stay above it. Artist and people with a deeper intellect see masterpieces for what they are and without influence. Trust that through your artistry, people will see youth truth. Remember, art will remain art even without human eulogies. You are a masterpiece and should spend time with people who see you as no less. Let me hear you say it, "I am a masterpiece!." .

"I am not what *happened* to me,
I am what I *choose* to become."

WRITE A LETTER TO YOUR YOUNGER SELF

One of the ways I have cultivated a healing and happy relationship with myself is by writing a letter to my younger self. It's a very powerful exercise that I hope all women reading this will do. We are surrounded by so much unknown as children that it's exciting, it's frightening, and it"s mystical. We grow up with our family members and educators telling us we can be anyone we want to be in the world, but that is only half the truth. They don't really elaborate on all of the blood, sweat, and tears it will take to become that person. So you're probably reminiscing about the times when your younger self was overwhelmed. You're thinking if she knew all that I know today, she would probably be at ease. Every time I write to my younger self, I remind her of her strength. She is stronger than she thinks. I make it a habit to inform her that there will be light at the end of her triumphs. Things get better and I need her to hang in there and continue to prevail. I release hurt, confusion, and anxiousness.

I wish I could hug her and let her know everything will turn out just fine. Although I am not able, I am satisfied with the fact that my writing this today will be living proof. What do you have to say to your younger self? Reason with the child in you. Heal the child in you.

"*Every* time you move forward,
make sure you give *back*."

GIVE BACK

*T*hroughout our matriculation of being students, we were never really taught about all of the possibilities out in the world once we enter adulthood. In one of Denzel Washington's commencement speeches, he said, "don't aspire to just make a living. Aspire to make a difference." Anything we want out of life that is fair, we can have it. We have to speak it into existence, we have to claim it, and we have to work hard to get it. Once we get it, it is in our hand to reach back and pull the next person up. That is the cycle we must keep afloat – giving back. We need to do a better job of instilling a culture where giving back is effortless. It needs to become such a social norm that everyone gives back because they want to. Giving back will be the core of change for our community and for our economy, but it starts with us. Blessed are the ones that are a blessing to others. No matter how major or minor, all simple acts of benevolence create the same impact. At the end of our life, it won't be about out how much we have accomplished. It'll be about who we have lifted up along the way, what we have given back, and who we have made a genuine impact on. Once we are on our feet, our work isn't done until we help someone else..

"We should be *inspired* by people who show that human beings can be kind and strong - even in the most *difficult* circumstances."

SAY SOMETHING NICE

I work in industries that thrive and flourish based on relationships and interactions. Some days I talk to many people, and some want to fully engage. On the other hand, there are others whom I speak, and it feels like I am talking to a cold brick wall. Some days people want to be left alone, and I understand that. Every day I strive to make sure I bring the same me and the same energy no matter what. I like to compliment people. I like to make others feel good about themselves. I find the value in that because I know when someone is having an off day it has less to do with me and more to do with what is currently going on in their life. Women have it hard! We never know the troubles and tribulations someone may be facing when they are not in the public eye. So it is always very important to be kind, smile, and it wouldn't hurt to throw out a compliment or two. That positive energy we are reflecting will return! I had a woman reach out to me on twitter who needed a few words of encouragement. I stopped what I was doing and took time to pray with her. That next morning she was telling me how much the prayers and positivity had resonated with her. She thought about taking her life that night, but it was the encouragement and kind words that brought her to another day. People have a way of always remembering how you help them feel. Make sure we are leaving these people better than we found them.

"Letting go never meant *loving* less."

WISH THEM WELL

*T*here are relationships I wish would've lasted my lifetime, but barely lasted five minutes. It's life. As we grow, we often forget that everything around us is growing as well. We outgrow people and surely enough people outgrow us. Each relationship we have ever invested in had purpose, and at one point it certainly felt good. When things go wrong, as they sometimes will, we don't always have to depart on bad terms. I had a friend in college who was nearly a sister to me. We were there for each other, confided in each other, but we didn't always see eye to eye. I thought the path she was on was dangerous, and after expressing that multiple times, I felt like my concerns were swept under the rug. Some of the things she put her energy into were toxic, and I could see it eating away at her potential. Don't get me wrong, I have my fair share of flaws, but when my friends point out some of my areas that need improvement, I make an effort to check myself. All I wanted was for all of us to continue to grow in a space where we could be our best selves, but she wasn't as on board as I would've liked. we grew apart because of this, but instead of having hate or any other ill feelings in my heart for her, I wished her well. I still genuinely wanted her to win whether we were friends or not. We have to be more conscious of not letting the shortcomings of relationships wear us down. Some people can't be helped, but to cringe when you hear their name is an unhealthy reaction.. For your sake and your sanity, when it doesn't work out with your loved ones, say your peace and wish them well. We don't need that lingering anger or illness on our hearts.

"A *wise* woman suggests that if you know one thing, it is that you know *nothing*."

REMAIN
COACHABLE

*T*ruly successful women know that even when they hit their highest peak of success, there is still much they have to learn. Less successful people want the acknowledgement of being "successful" before even learning enough to register how little they know. Did that riddle your brain as much as it riddled mine? When I have heard my managers, mentors, and coaches talk about me, they all say one of my greatest attributes is that I am coachable and always eager to know more. I think that is what separates truly successful people from mediocrity. The ones who are eager to know more tend to go further. Dig to find out what there is to know beyond what you're supposed to know. Everyday I am learning about the universe, my history, and my craft from people who are wise beyond my years. I consider it a blessing, and I am truly grateful that these individuals are able to pour so much knowledge into me. If we continue to be students of life, life will be limitless because knowledge is power. The more we know, the more comfortable and successful we will be navigating through the world. Even when you think you know all there is to know, I promise you there will be more to it. The only true wisdom subsides in the notion that if you know one thing it is nothing at all — remain coachable and remain a student of life.

"Do you *solemnly swear* to stay in your lane, your whole lane, and nothing but *your* lane?"

STAY IN YOUR LANE

*T*here is no competition when we are staying in our own lane. The only person we should be trying to be better than or one up on is the person we see every-day in the mirror. Our time to fully bloom is specific and will happen in due time, but for now let us put our sole focus into our growth – our personal development. I used to have a habit of jumping into things that didn't concern me. I admit! I have been involved with some people and things where their drama became my drama, I am in the middle of things, and now my energy is being exhausted on something that has absolutely nothing to do with me. If you can relate to this, you know that it's exhausting, and you know that it is just unnecessary. If you find yourself doing this, it's okay to check yourself. Tell yourself "that is not my lane" and adjust accordingly. Invest that energy into your own manifestation. Don't look to the other lane for validation on your progres-sion or to compare where others are on their journey with where you are.If we stay in our lane, we won't have to worry about traffic

"You will never *influence* the world by trying to be *like* the world."

OWN IT

Whatever difference you're making in any capacity, don't be ashamed to talk about it – post it if you want to! Own all of the light you are putting into the world and share it. I advise this for a few reasons. Social media has a way of kicking us content that doesn't wholesomely reflect all of the great qualities of what it means to be a woman. There's not enough empowerment, testimonials, and positive images of us just being the forces of nature that we are. When I get an opportunity to share something positive I am doing in the community, I do it with hopes that another young woman sees it and decides to make a difference within her community or within herself. Share your light. Own your light. It's not about using your platforms to brag about the work you do. It's about owning your light so that others will be motivated to share theirs as well. I see women harping on other women all of the time for publicizing their engagements. Motives are being questioned as if there is some type of hidden agenda behind sharing all of the good work that you do. I would rather the internet be flooded with accolades, service, and positivity. Nobody bats an eye when timelines are flooded with ratchet reality tv shows, school fights, and gossip blogs because media has made that the norm. That is what is entertaining. If we want to make a difference in how the world sees us, we have to make that change within our-selves. It all starts with owning your light and unapolo-getically sharing it with the universe.

"Don't get *confused* about what people say you can do and what you're actually *capable* of."

DO YOU

One day I stopped caring so much about what others thought about me, and I said to myself "do you?". According to the urban dictionary (I'm taking it there), "doing you" is the act of doing things that you would normally do or feel like doing without the consideration of opinions from anyone else. It's being yourself and showing everyone how unapologetic you are.. There comes a day in our lives when we have to cut the "crap" and do what makes our souls happy. One thing that sets us back from doing that in the first place is often times the criticism. Let me be the first to tell you that they may be asking why you're doing what you do, and soon after, they will be asking how. People used to double take when I told them I was writing a book or starting a nonprofit. How dare I dream that big? How dare you not? It's not your willingness to be yourself that pushes people away;. Sometimes it's their lack of being themselves.. Does that mean we should tone it down? No! Nobody wants to be constantly reminded about the shackles or box in which they've placed themselves. Do you and be a living, walking, and breathing example that you can break those chains and do as you please.

"Discover your *real* reason for being here and then have the courage to do something *with it*."

TAKE YOUR TIME

*I*n my early adulthood, I noticed most of my days were falling into some type of routine. I would wake up, go to work, come home, and take some time to work on me. This usually consisted of my following up with some administrative stuff, exercising, and writing this book. That's how I wanted to spend my time, but I knew in order to pay my bills every month and survive, there was a pecking order – work first. I didn't have a lot of time to watch TV, relax, and lay around. I had an interest in investing in myself and in order to do that I had to take my time. Not only take my time, but I decided how I was going to use that time – nobody else, but me. When you see potential in yourself, it urges you to build a foundation for that potential to grow. It takes time to build a foundation, but with a little consistency behind it that potential evolves into its full form. Along your journey, people will try to dictate what is a priority in your life, what they think you have time for, and even try to influence how you use your time. Don't let them. You and only you dictate what you will give your time to, and if you are genuinely invested in yourself, you will take your time seed, plant it, and reap the harvest.

"Loving yourself isn't *vanity* -
more like *sanity*."

AFFIRMATIVE ACTION

You owe yourself the love that you so generously give to other people. I hope one day you feel like a garden full of thriving daisies because of all of the self love and self care you have indulged in. Self love is the greatest kind of nourishment we can cultivate. What have you been doing lately to show yourself that you love you? Make a list of your good qualities. So many people spend a great deal of time giving voice to what they think is flaw, but rarely use that same energy to speak out on what is right or what is working. We have to counterbalance this. Give voice to your strengths, to the parts of you that you love, and start by writing it down on paper. When I can't think of any, I remember the times my loved ones have watered me with positive affirmations. I write those down. Temptation will try to provoke me to argue those points, but I won't give in. Accept them. Affirm all of the great qualities you know exist within and take a moment to read over them. Absorb these gentle thoughts and agree. Let the self love nourish and lather you like shea on the body.

"She who walks with the *wise*, grows wise. A companion of fools suffers *harm*."

REFLECTION
OF ME

By now I'm sure you're familiar with the saying "birds of a feather flock together." Essentially, we are a reflection of the company we keep. That's why it is wise to be very selective when choosing the people who surround us.. Growing up, my mother used to always warn me and tell me "not everyone is a friend, Bryann". As I went through life, I began to better understand what she meant and really appreciate the value of true friendship. Navigating through your teens and twenties gets difficult, and it feels a lot better when we have somebody by our side..The fact of the matter is there are people on our path that we grow through. We constantly want to be surrounding ourselves with people who lift us higher. Being in a questionable crowd will eventually influence us to start having questionable habits and make questionable decisions. I remember being the inhibiting friend that didn't contribute to anyone's growth. Then I remember the discontent when I realized I was "that girl". We are only going to be as good as the people with whom we surround ourselves.. Sometimes you have to cut off a few branches to save the tree. The incorporation of positive influences in our lives is absolutely necessary. The company we keep is also a reflection of how we see ourselves. Love yourself enough to make the necessary adjustments.

"What you *do* will always be louder
than what you *say*."

BELIEFS AND BEHAVIOR

Actions speak louder than words. We will come across people in our life that will serenade us with all the right things at just the right time, but if their actions do not coincide with what they are telling us, be wary. Beliefs do not make us better people, our behavior does. It's a perfect time to do some self assessment. Do your beliefs match your behavior? Is who you say you are the same person as who you actually are? The easiest way to get hurt is to believe what others tell you over what they show you. I remember to remind myself to believe them the first time they show me who they are even though I didn't always listen. There are those solid unwarranted feelings like love, care, and hope that stand in the way of our judgment. People may or may not always tell you how they feel about you, but they will show you. Believe that! All relations are sustained by behavior and action patterns of devotion noted in the things we say we're going to do and the things we actually do. The only way to discover a person's true character is not by listening to what they say, but observing what they do. What we do will always hold more weight than what we say.

"The *pessimist* complains about the wind; the optimist *expects* it to change; the realist adjust the *sails*."

CHANGE IS GOOD

Embracing change isn't always fun, but it doesn't necessarily have to be a bad thing. Comfort zones are safe - hence "comfort" zone. When I think of areas of comfort, I feel a sense of calm, security, and zen. All of a sudden life comes at us fast, and it comes along to stir things up. Things happen and change occurs, but that isn't anything out of the ordinary. This happens all the time. While some change is for the greater good, we can't help but feel the disruption and chaos in the midst of adjustments. Once I started looking at change as a positive experience, good things followed. In the realm of that, we are inheriting life skills that can be a major driver in our personal and professional life. It's not what happens to us, but it's the way we react to things that tell us a lot about who we are. Change reveals how truly powerful we are. I like to think of change as the wild flower that keeps life fresh. It breaks up routines and forces us to grow. Accepting change isn't as difficult as you think. It's often difficult to see change as easy when you're in the middle of it, but change is good. Change is a learning experience. Learning enables us to grow. To grow is to live. So live. Change is good.

"It's up to you to make your *mark* in this world, remain engaged, and adjust when it's time to *change* course."

IT'S NOT THE SIZE
OF THE BOAT

*I*t's not the size of the boat that determines how well it will sail, but it is the motion of the ocean and the will to venture. Are you willing to ride the waves? Will you let your boat venture from its anchor? Growing up and moving to California used to be the solve all for all things. I'm still not exactly sure why this was such a perception. . Keep in mind I'm from Minnesota which is surprisingly not as boring as you think! For some reason, there was an era where we all thought moving to California would move us one step closer to our dreams and a few steps further away from all of our problems. People had aspirations of being fashion designers, entertainers, pursuing an education, and and the list could get extensive. If you were like me, you just wanted to get as far away from the family troubles as you could. I thought the dysfunction of my home would inhibit me from growing and going anywhere .As grew up, I realized that success has no real association with where you start or what kind of home you grew up in, or your current environment. If we want to change our lives, it ultimately starts with our lifestyle. No matter where you were born, how you were reared, or where you are now, you can make a choice to do better and be better. Our psychological disposition will always hold value over our geographic locations. Pull your anchor up and ride the waves, because your boat will sail as long as you steer it.

"Strong winds mean *nothing* to a *wildflower* with strong roots."

DEEPLY ROOTED

*T*he woman you are becoming or growing to be will cost you. It will cost you friendships, relationships, opportunities, and sometimes even money. Keep choosing her over everything. The things we sacrifice for our growth will seem so small once we reach our biggest peak of growth. As we grow, our morality and beliefs tend to be nearer to our hearts. It becomes something that cannot be challenged. Our unwillingness to compromise will shake and stir some things up for your surroundings and people within it, but do not fold. Keep ten toes down and trust your intuition. What is real will grow with you. What is real will go with you. You may hear commentary on the new found glow radiating from your being, but don't get uncomfortable. That is the result of your "leveling up". Those are the results we want to see and feel. That is the type of feedback we should expect. When we are grounded in the idea of growth and keep the thoughts of elevation at our roots, we can only expect something revolutionary to happen. We can expect to see things blossoming along our branches. Today, we understand that all things come at a cost, even our growth. We accept it and sit still in our beliefs. We know that what is meant to be will be.

Acknowledgements:

GOD:

For I know that all things are possible by your mercy, grace, and favor. In 1 Corinthians 1:27 you told me that you choose the foolish things of the world to shame the wise - that you chose the weak things of the world to shame the strong. You never took your hand off of me, but instead decided to love me through it all. To the greatest love I've ever known, thank you.

ARDRE ORIE/13TH AND JOAN:

You have helped many women organize their thoughts in a fashion where they could bare their souls. I am so thankful to be one of those women. It has been a pleasure to be alongside a phenomenal force and girl boss in this authorship process. Thank you for expanding my vision and emboldening me to write fearlessly.

MY LOVE:

When I first told you I wanted to write a book, you never questioned my "why". You never talked me out of it.

You knew I had a story to tell. You instantly gave me the courage and the confidence to put the pen to the paper because you knew I was capable. It wasn't easy. I was isolated in my creativity, but when I reached back you were always there - before me, beside me. Thank you for watering me.

PARENTS:

I wouldn't go back in time and change a thing about our journey. Thank you both for doing the best you could to water me - even when our wells ran dry. How will we ever know how truly strong our roots are if there is no storm to weather? I love you.

GRANDMA:

When I was a little girl, I thought to myself "if I grew up to be half the woman she is, I know I will be okay". A strong woman full of love, light, and integrity. Thank you for the kind and caring way you've brought happiness into my world. Through the changing seasons, with your guidance I grew. I will always look at the flowers and see you. "Giddy up, giddy up, giddy up up up"

KIM AND GRETCH:

To my lifelong coach, mentor, and friend,
Thank you for believing in me when no one else did, but most importantly thank you for believing in me

when I didn't believe in myself. Thank you for giving me unconditional love and acceptance - even if it came in the form of cleaning out the storage closet.

MY SISTER CIRCLE:

Brittani, Chanell, Miriam, Dawii, Hailli, Maya, Laura,

God gave me living examples of resilience in the form of sisters. Your sisterhood is a gift generously given. You have filled my life with beauty, joy, and grace. Thank you for your support, constant inspiration, and for pushing me to be my best self. In the storms, you've covered me with your wings. In success, we shall raise our glass.

FAMILY:

Granny, Papa, Aunty Robin, and Aunty Leah:

Thank you for having ears that always listen and arms that always hold. Love is the greatest gift you could've given me, and I want to say thank you for always supplying your love and light no matter how near or far.

COUSIN CALVIN:

Play cousins are almost always better than real cousins, but blood couldn't make this bond any more unbreakable. I know you probably just read that first line and thought "bars", right? Thank you for the endless laughs, smiles, and support. When I told you I had aspirations of owning my own business, I came home to business development books on my doorstep. Thank you for supporting me in the most purest way possible.

JORDAN AND TROY:

To my best guy friends and partners in creativity,

Thank you for contributing to the advancement of both my personal and professional life. Thank you for believing in the hustle, but having all hands in when it came down to doing the work. You never had to, but you did out of the kindness of your heart and your belief in my dream.

RICHFIELD:

Thank you.

ABOUT THE
AUTHOR

*B*orn in Minnesota, Bryann Andrea's story of blossoming caught the nation's attention in 2017. Since then she's become a women's empowerment powerhouse. Bryann's untold story of overcoming some of the traumatic experiences in her women's journey is what motivated her to write *The Blossoming Woman*. She recognizes a need for creating spaces that allow women to not just survive, but thrive by using their truth. Bryann's goal as a philanthropist and branding maven is to create platforms that encourage all women to navigate their personal and professional careers with authenticity at the forefront.

Though the hardships of her early life stood as a formidable obstacle to her graduating high school, Bryann not only graduated, but received a scholarship to attend Shaw University.

There, she was given a chance to discover herself outside the bounds of her past. She planted seeds that bloomed into her decorated collegiate career as a highly respected student, athlete, entrepreneur, and advocate. In 2016 she graduated with her BA in Business Administration. Under the Obama administration, Bryann became the first student from Shaw University to be an ambassador for the Historical Black Colleges and Universities White House Initiatives (HBCU WHI).

She later became the Public Relations Director for the HBCU WHI Alumni Association, where she begin specializing in branding. That led to her current career as a sales representative within a Fortune 500 pharmaceutical company.

So, it's with honesty that Bryann admits to having stumbled upon her writing career. The more she grew as an entrepreneur, advocate, woman, and child of God, she realized her stories were not just for her. She felt a responsibility to help others plant seeds of truth, nurture their growth, and bloom. Bryann would share pieces of her journey across social media platforms where hundreds of women responded with gratitude because they too were growing through it. Since then, Bryann's literary work shed's light on loving oneself and using your story to teach, connect, and empower.

The Blôssoming Woman novel/book will be the foundation in a new age of women's empowerment that encourages all women to own their truth and use it to advance in their personal and professional careers.

CONNECT WITH BRYANN ANDREA AT

WWW.BRYANNANDREA.COM